Escape the 9-5: Embrace the Part-Time Revolution Design a Career You Love on Your Terms

By

Kristine J. Summers

Disclaimer:
The information provided in this book is for general informational purposes only. The author, Kristine J. Summers, is not liable for any damages or losses arising from the use of this information. Readers should consult with professionals for personalized advice and guidance tailored to their individual needs and circumstances.

About the Author

Kristine J. Summers is a dynamic content creator who thrives in the ever-evolving landscape of modern times. With a passion for storytelling and a keen eye for detail, Kristine crafts engaging and insightful content that resonates with audiences across various platforms.

Born and raised in a digital age, Kristine understands the importance of staying relevant and adaptable in today's fast-paced world. Drawing inspiration from her own experiences and the world around her, she brings a fresh perspective to her work, tackling topics ranging from lifestyle and personal development to entrepreneurship and career advancement.

As a content creator, Kristine is dedicated to creating meaningful and impactful content that inspires, informs, and entertains. Whether through blog posts, social media updates, or multimedia productions, she strives to connect with her audience on a deeper level, sparking conversations and fostering community along the way.

In addition to her creative pursuits, Kristine is a lifelong learner, constantly seeking out new opportunities for growth and self-improvement. With a curious mind and a thirst for knowledge, she embraces each day as an opportunity to learn, explore, and expand her horizons.

Table of Contents

Introduction:

Get out of the 9-to-5 grind and join the part-time revolution.

Are you sick of being stuck in a desk job from 9 to 5 every day? Do you wish you had more freedom, time, and flexibility in your life to do the things you love?

Millions of people around the world are giving up full-time jobs and joining the part-time movement. People in this trend want to have a better work-life balance, be financially independent, and be able to make their own careers that fit with their morals. Do you want to break out of the never-ending cycle of commuting, meeting goals, and having few leave days? A shocking 40% of people working now do independent work or work part-time, and it's not just to make extra money. Take Sarah as an example. She quit her job to have a free schedule that let her follow her love for photography and spend more time with her family. Is the 9-5 truly the only road to success? This book will explain the why and how behind the part-time change. It will also give you the tools and information to create a work life that supports your interests and makes you happy.

You wake up to the same loud alarm clock every morning, rush through breakfast, and then spend the next eight hours stuck to a desk, counting down the minutes until you can finally escape. Sound familiar?

Welcome to the world of the 9-5 grind! For generations, this has been the normal job model: clock in at 9, clock out at 5, repeat. But let's face it, this rigid plan comes with its limits. It leaves little room for freedom, stifles innovation, and often leads to burnout. But what if there was another way? What if you could break free from boredom and take control over your time and your life?
In this exploration, we will dig into the growing trend of part-time work, examining its benefits, challenges, and how it can empower you to create a more fulfilling and important life.

Gone are the days of hating Monday mornings and living for the weekends. With the Part-Time Revolution, every day becomes a chance to grow on your own terms. Imagine being able to plan work around your family commitments, hobbies, or personal projects. It's like having the power to create your dream lifestyle, one where work complements rather than consumes your life. And the best part? You're not alone in this journey. The Part-Time Revolution is a group movement, driven by people like you who refuse to settle for the status quo. Together, we're reshaping the landscape of work, accepting freedom, and clearing the way for a brighter, more satisfying future. So, whether you're a seasoned worker looking for a change or a recent learner eager to explore new possibilities, the Part-Time Revolution welcomes you with open arms. Get ready to start on a journey of freedom, innovation, and endless potential. The time to accept the Part-Time Revolution is now!

The 9-5 work model, where workers work a set routine of eight hours per day, Monday through Friday, has been the rule for decades. However, in recent times, its limits have become increasingly obvious.

Advantages:
Structure and predictability: The 9-5 plan provides a clear framework for work, which can be helpful for some people who thrive on routine and stability.
Collaboration and teamwork: Working set hours in a real place can help in-person contact and collaboration among coworkers.
Work-life separation: A defined work plan can help workers keep a clear distinction between work and personal life, which can be important for mental health and well-being.

Limitations:
Lack of flexibility: The rigid plan can be inflexible and incompatible with the needs of working parents, caregivers, or people with non-traditional schedules.
Commuting inefficiencies: Commuting to and from work can be time-consuming, expensive, and environmentally bad. Potential for burnout: Long hours sitting at a job can lead to fatigue, decreased output, and increased worry. Doesn't cater to different work styles: The 9-5 model believes that everyone is most effective during the same hours, which isn't always the case.

As technology and social norms change, alternative work arrangements are getting ground. These include:

Flexible work schedules: Allowing workers to work online, set their own hours, or compress their workday into fewer days. Part-time work: Providing chances for people to work fewer hours while still keeping a steady income.
The gig economy: Offering project-based work and freelance possibilities for those seeking more autonomy and control over their task.

The future of work is likely to be more open and adaptable, with a focus on results and output rather than simply the number of hours spent in the office. Companies that adopt innovative work models can draw and keep top talent, improve employee well-being, and boost total productivity.

While the 9-5 work model has served its purpose, it's important to recognize its limitations and explore alternative arrangements that better fit the needs of a diverse workforce and a changing world.

The standard 9-to-5 job is facing a challenge. Enter the part-time shift, a movement driven by a growing desire for freedom, liberty, and work-life balance. This change isn't just about working fewer hours; it's about changing work to fit the needs and goals of a diverse workforce.

Why is this happening?
Shifting priorities: Millennials and Gen Z value adventures and personal satisfaction alongside job success.
Technological advancements: Cloud computing, online communication tools, and automation allow work to be done from anywhere, anytime.
The rise of the gig economy: Platforms like Upwork and Fiverr offer project-based possibilities and casual work.
Burnout and dissatisfaction: Rigid plans and long hours are leading to employee burnout and a desire for a better work-life balance.

What does the part-time change look like?
Flexible work arrangements: Remote work, shortened workweeks, and job sharing are becoming increasingly popular.
Focus on results over hours: Companies are changing their focus to measuring efficiency and output rather than simply tracking time spent in the office.
The rise of the "portfolio career": Individuals are building jobs that mix part-time work, freelancing, and entrepreneurial projects.

Benefits of the part-time revolution:
Improved employee well-being: Reduced stress, better work-life balance, and greater job happiness.
Enhanced productivity: Employees can work during their most effective hours and escape the negative effects of burnout. Access to a bigger talent pool: Companies can draw and keep top talent regardless of

location or standard work plan limits. Environmental benefits: Reduced travel can lead to a smaller carbon impact.

Challenges and considerations: Ensuring effective communication and teamwork in virtual teams. Maintaining a good work-life balance when work and personal life limits cross. Potential for income insecurity in certain part-time or freelance jobs.

The part-time revolution is not a one-size-fits-all solution, but it marks a major shift in how we approach work. As technology and social norms continue to change, flexible work arrangements are likely to become the norm, enabling individuals to create jobs that fit with their interests and lives.

Welcome to the ultimate guidebook for breaking free from the 9-5 grind and jumping fully into the Part-Time Revolution! In this book, we'll be your trusty navigator as we start on a trip to explore the exciting world of flexible work arrangements. From the rise of part-time work to practical tips for finding the right gig, we've got you covered every step of the way.

First up, we'll dig into the evolution of work culture and discover the reasons behind the growing popularity of part-time work. Then, we'll dive into the benefits of accepting part-time work, from getting flexibility to following your passion projects. But hold on, we're not stopping there!

We'll also tackle head-on the stigma and misconceptions surrounding part-time work, providing you with the tools and strategies to beat any doubts or complaints. Next, we'll roll up our sleeves and get practical, with secret tips for handling the part-time job market like a pro.

But wait, there's more! We'll show you how to make part-time work not just sustainable but downright satisfying, with expert tips on handling funds, balancing multiple gigs, and avoiding burnout. And finally, we'll look into the crystal ball and explore the future of work, giving insights and predictions on what lies ahead in the ever-evolving world of employment.

So, whether you're a seasoned pro looking for a change or a fresh-faced learner eager to explore new possibilities, this book is your ticket to freedom, satisfaction, and a whole lot of fun. Get ready to leave the 9-5 and welcome the Part-Time Revolution like never before!

But hold onto your hats because this book isn't just about reading – it's about taking action and seizing control of your face. Along the way, we'll share inspiring stories of individuals who have successfully navigated the part-time landscape, showing that with drive and the right attitude, anything is possible.
So, grab a cup of coffee, cozy up in your best spot, and get ready to start on an adventure like no other. Whether you're dreaming of more time for family,

hobbies, or travel, the Part-Time Revolution is your guide to a life of freedom, flexibility, and happiness. Let's dive in and make your part-time dreams a reality!

Chapter One:

Rise of Part-Time Work:

Once upon a time, in the land of the 9-5, people lived by the clock, moving to the beat of a rigid workweek. But as the world changed, so did our ideas about work. Enter the rise of part-time employment – a game-changer that's changing up the standard work model and offering a new way of living and working.

Think of it as a breath of fresh air in a hot room. Part-time work is all about flexibility, giving people the freedom to choose when and where they work. Whether it's parents handling childcare, students mixing studies with a job, or retirees easing into a slower pace of life, part-time work opens doors for people of all walks of life.

But why the quick surge in popularity? Well, let's take a closer look. For starters, technology has made it easier than ever to work online, breaking down the barriers of the standard office and paving the way for flexible plans. Plus, with the gig economy on the rise, more and more companies are turning to part-time workers to fill their staffing needs, giving chances for side hustles and extra income.

But it's not just about ease – there's a deeper shift going in the way we view work. Part-time work isn't just about punching the clock; it's about finding balance, following passions, and living life to the best. It's about valuing well-being over burnout and accepting a more holistic approach to work and life.

So, as we bid farewell to the old 9-5 and accept the start of the part-time change, one thing is clear: the future of work is flexible, and the options are endless. Whether you're a leader making your own path or a skeptic still on the fence, there's no denying that part-time work is here to stay – and it's changing the way we live, work, and thrive.

1. Exploring the Evolution of Work Culture

Once upon a time, work was like a well-oiled machine – everyone had their place, their hours, and their tasks. But as time marched on and society changed, so too did the way we work. It was a gradual shift, marked by times of creativity, revolt, and adaptation.

Long gone are the days when a job meant living your entire life at the same company, climbing the corporate ladder one rung at a time. Instead, we find ourselves in a world where change is the only constant, and adaptation is key.

So, what caused this change of work culture? Well, it's a tale as old as time, really. As technology advanced, borders blurred, and the global economy became increasingly interconnected, the standard 9-5 model started to feel more like a relic of the past than a plan for the future.

People began to crave more flexibility in their lives – the freedom to work when and where they wanted, to follow their passions alongside their jobs, and to value family and personal time without sacrificing their professional ambitions.

And thus, the rise of part-time work started. It wasn't just a job – it was a lifestyle, an attitude, a revolt against the status quo. Part-time work gave the best of both worlds: the security of steady pay mixed with the freedom to chart your own path.

But it wasn't just people causing this shift – companies, too, began to understand the benefits of embracing flexibility in the workplace. By giving part-time jobs, they could tap into a bigger talent pool, keep top performers, and adapt more quickly to changing market conditions.

And so, as we stand on the brink of a new era in work culture, let us enjoy the progress that has brought us here. Let us accept the freedom, flexibility, and satisfaction that part-time work offers. After all, in a world where the only constant is change, why stick to the past when the future is so full of possibility?

As the evolution of work culture continues, driven by technological advancements and changing societal norms, the rise of part-time employment is set to reshape the way we think about work.

One of the driving reasons behind this development is the changing nature of work itself. In today's fast-paced world, where innovation is the name of the game and businesses are constantly evolving, the standard 9-5 model no longer fits the bill. Companies need to be flexible, adaptable, and sensitive to stay ahead of the curve, and part-time work offers them the freedom to do just that.

Moreover, the rise of part-time employment represents a wider culture shift towards valuing work-life balance and prioritizing personal satisfaction over standard markers of success. People are no longer happy to trade their health, happiness, and relationships for the sake of a paycheck. Instead, they're seeking out chances that allow them to lead more healthy, worthwhile lives – and part-time work is the right answer.

But perhaps the most convincing reason behind the rise of part-time jobs is the undeniable fact that it works. Studies have shown that part-time workers are often just as effective – if not more so – than their full-time peers. By giving workers greater autonomy and freedom, businesses can unlock higher levels of creativity, innovation, and engagement, leading to better results for everyone involved.

So, as we continue to study the evolution of work culture and the reasons behind the rise of part-time employment, let us welcome the possibilities that lie ahead. Let us reimagine the way we work, value flexibility and balance, and build a world where everyone has the freedom to thrive – both personally and professionally. After all, the time for change is now, and the Part-Time Revolution is showing the way!

The rise of part-time work can be linked to several key factors:

1. Flexibility: Many people, especially parents, caregivers, and students, seek part-time work to suit their personal responsibilities and schedules. Part-time jobs help them to strike a balance between work and other responsibilities.

2. Work-life balance: In today's fast-paced world, more people are prioritizing their personal well-being and finding jobs that give a better work-life balance. Part-time work gives the flexibility to explore hobbies, spend time with family, and keep a healthy lifestyle.

3. Changing views towards work: There's a rising awareness that long hours and overwork are not realistic or beneficial to general happiness and efficiency. Part-time employment offers an option to the standard 9-5 grind, allowing individuals to work fewer hours while still making a living.

4. Technological advancements: The rise of technology has made it easier than ever for people to work online or on a free schedule. With tools like video conferencing, cloud computing, and project

management software, people can perform their jobs effectively from anywhere, making part-time plans more possible.

5. Gig economy: The gig economy, defined by short-term contracts and freelance work, has added to the rise of part-time jobs. Many people choose to work part-time as independent contractors or freelancers, taking on multiple gigs to diversify their income and follow their hobbies.

6. Employer flexibility: Employers are increasingly understanding the benefits of having part-time jobs. Part-time employees can bring important skills and knowledge to the table, and hiring part-time workers allows companies to adjust staffing numbers based on demand and control labor costs.

7. Economic factors: In some cases, part-time work comes from economic necessity. With rising living costs and low pay in certain industries, individuals may need to boost their income with part-time work to make ends meet. Part-time employment gives a way for people to create extra income without committing to full-time hours.

8. Career transitions: Part-time work can also serve as a stepping stone for people moving between careers or industries. It allows them to gain experience, test out different jobs, and explore new possibilities without fully committing to a standard full-time job. This freedom can be especially helpful

for those looking to pivot their jobs or follow passion projects.

9. Demographic shifts: As demographics change, with an older population and a growing number of retirees, there is a rising demand for part-time job possibilities. Many retirees choose to work part-time as a way to stay busy, involved, and boost their retirement income. Similarly, younger generations may opt for part-time work to gain experience and financial independence while pursuing schooling or other hobbies.

10. Legal and regulatory changes: Changes in labor laws and regulations can also affect the prevalence of part-time work. In some cases, government policies may incentivize or require companies to offer part-time choices, such as flexible work arrangements or reduced hours, to promote work-life balance and support diverse workforce needs.

Overall, the rise of part-time work represents a complicated interplay of human preferences, economic dynamics, technological advances, and societal changes. It provides people with greater freedom, employers with more agile staffing choices, and society with chances for inclusivity and diversity in the workforce. As the world of work continues to change, part-time employment is likely to remain a prominent feature, giving a realistic and attractive option to standard full-time jobs.

2. Statistics and Trends Highlighting the Rise of Part-Time Work

The popularity of part-time work is clearly on the rise, driven by a confluence of social, technological, and economic factors. Here's a breakdown of key data and trends:

1. Increased Part-Time Employment Rates: Over the past decade, there has been a steady increase in the percentage of part-time workers in the workforce. According to statistics from the Bureau of Labor Statistics (BLS) in the United States, the percentage of part-time workers has been rising steadily, with roughly 18-20% of the workforce being worked part-time.

2. Rise of the Gig Economy: The gig economy, characterized by short-term contracts and freelance work, has added greatly to the rise of part-time jobs. Platforms like Uber, Lyft, and TaskRabbit have allowed individuals to work part-time on their own terms, adding to the general rise in part-time employment.

3. Flexibility in the Workplace: Many companies are understanding the benefits of having flexible work plans, including part-time choices, to attract and keep talent. According to a study by the Society for Human Resource Management (SHRM), 83% of HR workers claimed that their organizations offered some form of flexible work arrangements, including part-time schedules.

4. Desire for Work-Life Balance: Surveys consistently show that work-life balance is a top concern for workers. According to Gallup's State of the American Workplace study, 53% of employees say that a role that allows them to have better work-life balance is "very important" to them when choosing a job. Part-time work gives people the flexibility to balance work with personal responsibilities and hobbies.

5. Demographic Shifts: As demographics change, with more millennials joining the workforce and older adults delaying retirement, there is a growing demand for part-time job choices. Many millennials value freedom and liberty in their work arrangements, while older people may seek part-time work as a way to stay active and support their retirement income.

6. Impact of COVID-19: The COVID-19 pandemic has increased the acceptance of remote work and flexible work plans, including part-time choices. Many companies moved to online work during the pandemic, leading to greater acceptance of non-traditional work arrangements. Additionally, some people may have moved to part-time work as a result of job loss or changes in their personal situations during the pandemic.

7. Industry Trends: Certain industries have seen a notable rise in the frequency of part-time work. For example, the retail and leisure sectors commonly

depend on part-time workers to handle fluctuating demand, yearly peaks, and irregular schedules. Similarly, the healthcare business often gives part-time jobs to handle staff shortages and provide coverage during off-peak hours.

8. Educational Pursuits: Part-time employment is also popular among students and people seeking further education. Many students work part-time to support themselves financially while attending school, getting important work experience and cash without sacrificing their studies. Likewise, people going to school for job growth or personal development often opt for part-time employment to balance their academic and professional duties.

9. Remote Work possibilities: The rise of remote work has expanded the availability of part-time job possibilities, especially for people wanting remote or telecommuting roles. Remote part-time jobs offer the freedom to work from anywhere, removing physical limits and allowing people to choose when and where they work.

10. Entrepreneurship and Side Hustles: Part-time work is also popular among prospective entrepreneurs and individuals seeking side hustles. Many people work part-time while building their own businesses or pursuing artistic projects, using part-time employment as a source of income and security while following their entrepreneurial dreams.

11. Global Trends: The rise of part-time work is not limited to specific regions or countries but is noticed on a global scale. Countries around the world are facing similar shifts in work culture, with part-time employment becoming increasingly common as people seek greater freedom, autonomy, and work-life balance.

12. Shift in Employer Practices: Employers are adapting their hiring practices to meet the changing wants and desires of the workforce. Many businesses are accepting part-time work as a strategic approach to people management, recognizing that having flexible work arrangements can enhance recruitment efforts and improve employee happiness and retention rates.

13. Impact of Automation and AI: The rise of automation and artificial intelligence (AI) has led to the creation of new job roles and skill needs, changing the nature of work. Part-time employment gives people the chance to adapt to these changes by gaining useful skills and experience while keeping a flexible work schedule.

14. Culture Shifts: There has been a culture change towards valuing experiences over material goods, with many individuals choosing lifestyle choices and personal satisfaction over standard job routes. Part-time work aligns with this shift, allowing people to follow their interests, spend time with loved ones,

and participate in leisure activities while still making cash.

15. Growing Awareness of Work-Related Stress: Increased knowledge of the negative effects of work-related stress and burnout has pushed people to seek alternative work arrangements that value their well-being. Part-time employment offers a reduced task and more manageable work hours, helping people avoid the pitfalls of overwork and keep a healthy work-life balance.

16. Changing Definitions of Career Success: The meaning of career success is changing, with many people putting greater stress on personal satisfaction, purpose, and work-life integration rather than standard markers of success such as pay or job title. Part-time work allows people to customize their jobs to align with their values, hobbies, and life goals.

The rise of part-time work is likely to continue, driven by technological breakthroughs, evolving workplace cultures, and changing employee tastes. Businesses will need to adapt by giving flexible work arrangements, online work options, and reduced perks to draw and keep talent. Additionally, social safety nets and portable benefits systems may be necessary to handle the issues associated with part-time work.

The data and trends paint a clear picture: part-time work is no longer a marginal event, but a growing force shaping the future of work. As we move forward, it's crucial to build a work environment that caters to the needs of a diverse workforce, giving flexibility, security, and chances for growth, regardless of job status.

3. Benefits and Challenges Associated with Part-time Employment.

Benefits of Part-Time Employment:

1. Freedom: Part-time work gives people the freedom to match work with personal duties, such as parenting tasks, education, or following hobbies and interests. This flexibility makes for a better work-life mix and can help to general well-being.

2. Work-Life Balance: Part-time employment can help people achieve a healthier work-life balance by allowing them to allocate more time to family, friends, and personal interests. This balance can lower stress, increase job satisfaction, and improve general quality of life.

3. Diverse Possibilities: Part-time work gives access to a wide range of job possibilities in various businesses and sectors. This variety helps people to explore different jobs, learn new skills, and expand their professional networks.

4. Financial Supplement: Part-time work can supplement income from other sources, such as a

full-time job, stocks, or retirement savings. This extra income can help individuals meet financial goals, cover living costs, and save for the future.

5. Career Development: Part-time work gives chances for career development and advancement, allowing people to gain useful experience, build skills, and show their capabilities to possible employers. Part-time jobs can serve as stepping stones to full-time roles or higher-level positions within a company.

6. Decreased Commute Time: Working part-time often includes fewer hours in the office, resulting in decreased commute times and transportation costs. This time savings can add to a better work-life balance and provide individuals with more time to focus on other responsibilities.

7. Work-Life Integration: Part-time employment helps people to integrate their work responsibilities more seamlessly into their personal lives. With fewer hours committed to work, part-time employees have more time and energy to give to family, hobbies, and other interests. This merging can lead to greater general happiness and fulfillment, as people are better able to keep a healthy balance between work and non-work activities.

8. Reduced Stress: Part-time work can lead to reduced stress levels compared to full-time job. With fewer hours spent working, part-time workers may

experience less burnout, fatigue, and mental pressure connected with long work hours. This lessened stress can lead to better mental health and well-being, as people have more time for self-care and relaxation.

9. Career Flexibility: Part-time work gives people greater flexibility to follow alternative career paths and explore different possibilities. By working part-time, people can gain exposure to various industries, jobs, and work environments, allowing them to find their interests, skills, and passions. This work flexibility can lead to improved job happiness and fulfillment over the long run.

10. Personal Development: Part-time work offers chances for personal growth and development outside of the traditional job. With more time available for self-improvement activities, part-time employees can explore further education, training, or skill-building projects to increase their professional competencies and expand their job horizons. This personal growth can lead to greater confidence, resilience, and adaptability in the face of future difficulties.

11. Improved Health and Well-being: Part-time work may lead to improved physical and mental health outcomes for people. With more time available for rest, exercise, and leisure activities, part-time employees may experience better general health, decreased chance of chronic diseases, and improved life satisfaction. This better health and well-being can

positively impact all areas of life, from personal relationships to work performance.

12. Social Connections: Part-time work offers chances for social contact and relationships with colleagues and peers. While part-time employees may spend fewer hours in the workplace, they still have the chance to build important relationships, collaborate on projects, and join in team activities. These social ties can promote a sense of belonging, camaraderie, and support within the work setting.

13. Diverse Experiences: Part-time work exposes people to diverse experiences, views, and obstacles that can improve their career and personal lives. By working part-time, individuals may have the chance to connect with people from different backgrounds, nations, and businesses, increasing their views and growing their viewpoint. This exposure to variety can improve creativity, innovation, and problem-solving skills in the workplace.

14. Transition Opportunities: Part-time work can serve as a transitional step for people navigating life changes or job transitions. Whether returning to the workforce after a break, moving to retirement, or exploring new options, part-time work offers a flexible and low-pressure environment to ease into changes gradually. This transition phase can provide security, financial support, and a feeling of purpose during times of uncertainty or shift.

Overall, the benefits of part-time employment stretch far beyond financial considerations, covering aspects of work-life balance, personal growth, health and well-being, social ties, and job freedom. By leveraging these benefits, individuals can create a work plan that matches with their values, goals, and ambitions, leading to greater happiness and success in both their working and personal lives.

Challenges of Part-Time Employment:

1. Limited Benefits: Part-time employees may not have access to the same benefits and perks as full-time workers, such as health insurance, retirement plans, paid time off, and career development chances. This lack of benefits can impact financial security and general job happiness.

2. Income Instability: Part-time employment may be defined by irregular or unpredictable income, based on factors such as hours worked, yearly fluctuations, and changes in demand. This income instability can make it difficult to budget and plan for costs.

3. Limited Career Advancement: Part-time workers may face obstacles to career advancement, as they may be missed for raises or chances for growth compared to their full-time peers. Limited access to training, networking, and mentorship programs can further hinder job advancement.

4. Workload Imbalance: Part-time employees may experience an imbalance in workload, with tasks and duties often being shifted to full-time staff during busy times or high-demand projects. This imbalance can lead to feelings of injustice and unhappiness among part-time workers.

5. Social Isolation: Part-time employees may feel socially isolated or disconnected from their coworkers, as they may not have the same chances for teamwork, networking, and social contact as full-time workers. This lack of connection can harm job happiness and engagement.

6. Limited Job Security: Part-time employment may offer less job security than full-time roles, as part-time workers may be more subject to cuts, reductions in hours, or changes in employment status during economic downturns or organizational restructuring.

7. Difficulty in improving Skills: Part-time employees may face hurdles in improving their skills and knowledge compared to full-time workers. Limited access to training, professional development opportunities, and mentoring programs can hinder skill development and job growth, possibly hurting long-term employment and income potential.

8. Stigma and Perceptions: Part-time work is sometimes viewed as less prestigious or useful compared to full-time job. Part-time workers may face

stigma or bad views from others, including bosses, coworkers, and society at large, which can impact self-esteem and job happiness.

9. Lack of Security: Part-time employment may lack the security and predictability of full-time jobs, as part-time workers may be subject to changes in schedule, hours, or shifts based on organizational needs or fluctuations in demand. This lack of stability can cause uncertainty and anxiety about future job possibilities.

10. Difficulty in Securing Benefits: Part-time workers may face challenges in obtaining important benefits such as health insurance, retirement plans, and paid time off. Many companies keep these perks for full-time workers, leaving part-time employees vulnerable to financial strain and inadequate healthcare coverage.

11. Legal Protections: Part-time workers may have fewer legal protections and rights compared to full-time employees, especially in areas such as employment discrimination, wage and hour rules, and job stability. This lack of legal safeguards can leave part-time workers exposed to exploitation or unfair treatment in the workplace.

12. Workload Overload: In some cases, part-time workers may be expected to take on additional tasks or work beyond their planned hours to meet organizational demands. This task overload can lead

to burnout, worry, and dissatisfaction among part-time workers, undermining the benefits of flexible work plans.

13. Career Trajectory: Part-time employment may impact long-term career trajectories and chances for growth, as part-time workers may be viewed as less committed or less capable compared to their full-time peers. This impression can limit professional growth and limit access to higher-paying or more senior roles in the future.

14. Health and Well-being: Part-time employment may have effects for physical and mental health outcomes, as part-time workers may experience higher levels of worry, anxiety, and job insecurity compared to full-time employees. This can impact general well-being and quality of life for part-time workers and their families.

15. Limited Networking Chances: Part-time employees may have fewer chances to network, build professional relationships, and access job development tools compared to full-time workers. This limited access to networking opportunities can hinder career growth and limit access to job opportunities in the future.

Despite these difficulties, many people find fulfillment and satisfaction in part-time work, leveraging its benefits to achieve their personal and professional goals. By solving these challenges and pushing for policies and practices that support part-time workers, organizations can create more open and helpful work settings for all employees.

Overall, while part-time work offers many benefits, it also presents difficulties that people must navigate to achieve success and satisfaction in their jobs. By knowing and solving these challenges, both employees and companies can create more helpful and open work settings for part-time workers.

Chapter Two:

Embracing Part-Time Work: A Win-Win for Individuals and Organizations

In an era where flexibility and work-life balance are increasingly valued, part-time work has appeared as a powerful choice for a wide range of people. Offering a unique mix of cash gain and personal freedom, part-time jobs cater to diverse wants and ambitions. Whether you're a student, a parent, or someone wanting a job change, part-time work unlocks a treasure trove of advantages that can enrich your life both individually and professionally.

While the flexibility of part-time scheduling is a well-known advantage, the benefits stretch far beyond simply having extra free time. Let's dig deeper and study the multifaceted value offer of part-time work:

Flexibility: Part-time schedules often provide the freedom to choose working hours that fit with your current commitments. This can be a game-changer for students handling studies, parents attending to babysitting needs, or individuals following other interests alongside work.

Financial Boost: A part-time job can be a useful source of income, helping you cover costs, save for future goals, or even gain financial independence.

This extra income can provide a much-needed cushion or open doors to new chances.
Skill Development: Even part-time roles offer important chances to learn and grow professionally. You can learn new skills, enhance current ones, and build a strong work ethic. This can be especially helpful for students joining the workforce or those looking to transition careers.

Work-Life Balance: Part-time work helps you to strike a good balance between your career and home life. With more free time, you can prioritize hobbies, spend time with loved ones, or explore personal interests, leading to reduced stress and better overall well-being.

Networking Opportunities: Part-time jobs can connect you with new people and expand your career network. You can interact with colleagues, mentors, and industry pros, possibly membuka new doors to future job possibilities.

Exploration and Experimentation: For those unsure about their job path, part-time work in different areas can provide useful insights and help you find your hobbies and interests. This low-risk method allows you to explore different options before committing to a full-time career.

Reduced Stress and Improved Well-being: With fewer work hours, part-time jobs can help alleviate the pressure and stress connected with full-time roles.

This can lead to a better lifestyle, greater mental focus, and a more upbeat attitude.
Stepping Stone to Full-time: Part-time work can sometimes act as a stepping stone to full-time possibilities within the same company. By showing your skills and work ethic, you can increase your chances of being considered for more permanent jobs.

Part-time work is more than just a paycheck; it's a strategic tool that allows you to shape your life according to your interests and goals.

The traditional full-time work plan is no longer the only way to success. Part-time work is getting momentum, giving a compelling option for both people and groups. Let's explore the variety of benefits that accepting part-time work brings to the table.

1. Benefits for Individuals

1. Enhanced Work-Life Balance:
Part-time schedules help people to build a harmonious blend of work and personal responsibilities.

The traditional full-time work approach can often feel like a constant tug-of-war between business responsibilities and personal well-being. Part-time work offers a powerful answer, allowing people to build a more balanced and satisfying life. This can lead to decreased stress, better mental and physical well-being, and more time for family, hobbies, or self-care.

Here's how:
Reduced Stress and Improved Mental Health: By reducing work hours, part-time workers experience less pressure and stress compared to their full-time peers. This can greatly lower stress levels, leading to better emotional well-being and a sense of control over their time.

More Time for Family and Relationships: Part-time work helps people to dedicate valuable time to their loved ones. This could mean visiting children's school events, caring for elderly parents, or simply having evenings and weekends together. Stronger family ties and a helpful network add to general happiness and mental well-being.

Prioritizing Self-Care and Personal Growth: With extra time in their hands, people can focus on activities that feed their mind, body, and spirit. This might include following hobbies and interests, moving regularly, getting enough sleep, or helping in their communities. Investing in self-care leads to increased energy, better happiness, and a greater sense of purpose.

Flexibility for Personal Needs: Life throws curveballs, and part-time work gives the agility to handle them. Whether it's having doctor's visits, handling unexpected situations, or simply needing a mental health day, part-time schedules offer the freedom to handle personal needs without jeopardizing job stability.

Striking a Balance Between Work and Passion: For individuals who are passionate about activities outside of their work, part-time plans allow them to devote time to these efforts. This could involve starting a side hustle, exploring creative projects, or simply having the mental space to explore new hobbies.

Part-time work enables people to become the architects of their own work-life balance. It's not just about having more free time; it's about having the control and freedom to build a life that is personally fulfilling and professionally satisfying.

2. Financial Flexibility:
While the financial boost from part-time work is obvious, its benefits stretch far beyond simply adding extra zeros to your paycheck.

Part-time work offers a valuable source of income to supplement current earnings, save for future goals, or handle debt. It's particularly helpful for students, parents, or those wanting extra financial security.

Here's how:
Empowering Financial freedom: Part-time income can be a game-changer, especially for students, single parents, or people wanting financial freedom. It allows you to cover everyday costs, save for future goals like

a dream trip or a down payment on a house, or even pay off debt and achieve greater financial security.

Building a Safety Net: Part-time work provides a valuable cushion against unexpected financial problems. Whether it's a car repair, medical bill, or any unexpected event, having a backup source of income can offer peace of mind and help you manage difficult situations without financial pressure.

Investing in Yourself: The extra income from part-time work can be used to invest in your personal and career growth. This could include taking classes or workshops to improve your skills, seeking certifications to advance your job, or visiting conferences to network and gain industry knowledge.

Exploring Entrepreneurial Ventures: Part-time work can serve as a start for beginning your own business. The extra income allows you to test the waters of your business idea, gain useful experience, and build a customer base before taking the leap to full-time entrepreneurship.

Learning Financial Management: Juggling income from two sources can be an excellent chance to improve your financial management skills. You can learn to budget successfully, prioritize spending, and create healthy saving habits that benefit you in the long run.

Boosting Self-Confidence: Earning your own income, handling your finances effectively, and meeting financial goals can significantly boost your self-confidence and sense of success. This newfound financial freedom empowers you to make educated choices and take control of your future.

Part-time work is more than just a paycheck; it's a tool for achieving financial security, building a safety net, and investing in your personal and professional growth. It empowers you to take care of your funds and pave the way for a better financial future.

3. Skill Development and Career Exploration: Part-time jobs offer chances to gain important work experience, learn new skills, and broaden professional networks. This can be a stepping stone to full-time jobs or a way to explore different career routes without a full-time commitment.

Part-time work isn't just about making extra cash; it's a springboard for starting and propelling your job forward.

Here's how:
Gaining Valuable Work knowledge: Even part-time jobs offer real-world knowledge that goes straight to your resume. You'll learn important job skills like communication, teamwork, problem-solving, and time management. This training makes you a more attractive candidate for future full-time jobs.

Developing a Diverse Sk ll Set: Part-time work allows you to explore different industries and jobs, giving you the chance to acquire new skills that suit your current skill set. This can make you a more versatile and adaptable option in the work market.

Building Your Professional Network: Every workplace contact is a possible networking chance. Through part-time work, you'll meet colleagues, teachers, and industry professionals who can provide useful advice, support your career goals, and even open doors to future job chances.

Testing the Waters of Different Careers: Unsure of your ideal job path? Part-time work allows you to experiment with different areas without a full-time commitment. This "try before you buy" method helps you discover your passions, measure your strengths and weaknesses, and make informed choices about your future job direction.

Transitioning to Full-Time Opportunities: Part-time work can be a stepping stone to a full-time job within the same company. Your strong work ethic, positive attitude, and the skills you build can please your boss, making you a natural choice for a full-time opening.

Staying Relevant in the Workforce: During job breaks or while seeking higher education, part-time work helps you to stay connected to your field and maintain your professional skills. This keeps your resume updated and makes it easier to re-enter the job when you're ready.

Building Confidence and Self-Belief: Successfully navigating the workplace, learning new skills, and overcoming obstacles all add to a strong sense of success and self-belief. This newfound confidence shines through in job interviews and future work efforts.

Part-time work is an investment in your career growth. It equips you with important knowledge, skills, and contacts, paving the way for a successful and fulfilling work journey.

4. Education and Training:
Part-time work allows people to seek educational options or training programs alongside their job. This can lead to job advancement or a full career change; it can be a powerful tool for lifelong learning and career advancement.

Here's how:
Funding Your Education: Part-time work can help you meet the prices of tuition, books, and other educational bills. This helps you to continue higher education or professional training programs without taking on excessive debt.

Flexible Learning Options: Many educational institutions offer online courses, evening classes, or part-time programs that cater to working people. This freedom allows you to juggle your work obligations with your studies.

Developing Applicable Skills: The skills you learn from your part-time job can directly support your schooling. For instance, working in customer service can enhance your conversation and interpersonal skills, while working in an office job can improve your organizational and time management abilities.

Networking chances: Educational schools and training programs often provide chances to connect with classmates, teachers, and industry pros. This networking can lead to useful business advice, job suggestions, and possible mentorship possibilities.

Putting Theory into Practice: The knowledge and skills you learn in your studies can be applied straight to your part-time work. This real experience solidifies your learning and shows your capabilities to possible employers.

Career Changers: Part-time work in your chosen field can be a strategic way to gain useful experience while pursuing the necessary schooling or training. This combination can significantly improve your chances of landing a full-time job in your new work path.

Staying Up-to-Date: In today's fast changing job market, constant learning is important. Part-time work allows you to stay current with industry trends and developments while seeking appropriate training or certifications. This makes you relevant and in demand.

By carefully combining part-time work with your
educational goals, you can create a strong synergy
that fuels your professional growth and opens doors
to interesting job possibilities.

5. Reduced Stress and Improved Health:
By avoiding work stress and burnout, part-time
workers can value their mental and physical health.
This can lead to a more balanced and satisfying living.

The constant pressure of a full-time job can take a toll
on your well-being. Part-time work offers a nice
break, promoting a healthier and happier lifestyle in
several ways:

Reduced Stress and Anxiety: By reducing work hours,
part-time workers experience less pressure and
workload, leading to a significant drop in stress and
anxiety levels. This can improve your mood, sleep
quality, and general feeling of well-being.

Improved Work-Life Balance: Part-time plans allow
you to give more time to activities that reduce stress
and promote relaxing, such as spending time with
loved ones, following hobbies, or participating in
physical exercise.

Prioritizing Physical Health: With more free time, you
have the chance to focus on your physical health. This
could involve exercising regularly, eating nutritious
meals, and getting enough sleep – all important for
keeping good health and avoiding chronic diseases.

Enhanced Mental Clarity: The mental break given by part-time work helps your mind to recover and de-clutter. This can lead to improved attention, greater creativity, and better decision-making skills.

Greater Control and Autonomy: Part-time work often offers more freedom in schedule and task. This sense of control over your work life can empower you and add to a feeling of accomplishment and happiness.

Reduced Risk of Burnout: By avoiding work overload, part-time workers are less subject to burnout, a state of mental tiredness, negativity, and reduced effectiveness. This saves your mental health and general well-being.

Part-time work isn't just about working less; it's about working better. It allows you to build a more sustainable work-life balance, value your health and well-being, and eventually lead a happier and more rewarding life.

6. Retirees Stay Active and Engaged:
Part-time work offers seniors a feeling of purpose, social contact, and continued intellectual stimulation. It's a fantastic way to stay linked to the community and keep a feeling of accomplishment.

Retirement is no longer linked with rocking chairs and lazy days. Part-time work gives retirees a special chance to stay busy, involved, and connected, enriching their golden years in several ways:

Combating Boredom and Loneliness: The structure and routine of part-time work can help seniors avoid feelings of boredom and isolation that can sometimes follow retirement. Social contact with workers and customers provides a sense of belonging and combats feelings of loneliness.

Maintaining Purpose and Identity: Work often gives a feeling of purpose and identity. Part-time jobs help retirees to continue using their skills and experience, adding to society, and feeling valuable.

Mental Stimulation and Cognitive Benefits: Engaging in new tasks and learning new skills through part-time work can help keep retired mentally sharp and improve cognitive function. This can help fight off age-related decline and boost mental well-being.

Financial Security and Independence: Part-time work can boost retirement income, allowing seniors to keep their desired lifestyle, handle unexpected costs, or even explore travel and hobbies.

Social Connection and Community Engagement: The workplace offers chances to engage with people of all ages and backgrounds. This social interaction helps retirees stay linked to their communities and fight feelings of isolation.

Sense of success and Contribution: Successfully finishing chores and adding to a team effort provides seniors with a sense of success and self-worth, improving their confidence and general well-being.

Part-time work isn't just about making extra cash; it's about enjoying a happy and active retirement lifestyle. It helps retirees to stay mentally and socially stimulated, linked to their communities, and feeling valuable members of society.

2. Benefits for Organizations

The traditional full-time workforce strategy is no longer the main answer for businesses. Here's how accepting part-time work can create a win-win situation for organizations:

1. Access to a Wider Talent Pool:
By giving part-time positions, groups can tap into a wider range of skilled people who may not be available for full-time commitments. This includes students, parents, retired, and those with specific skills.

Students: Gain useful work experience while balancing studies.

Parents: Achieve work-life balance while offering their skills and knowledge.

Retirees: Offer experienced workers and new views. Individuals with Specialized Skills: Provide special knowledge on a project-by-project basis.

2. Cost-Effectiveness:
Part-time workers generally require fewer benefits compared to full-time staff, leading to possible cost savings on salaries, healthcare, and other benefits. Additionally, companies can scale their staff up or down based on seasonal needs or project requirements, optimizing labor costs.

3. Increased Efficiency and Productivity: Studies have shown that part-time workers can be highly focused and efficient due to their shorter work hours. They may bring a fresh viewpoint and novel ideas to the table, promoting a dynamic work environment.

4. Improved Talent Retention: Offering part-time work shows an employer's dedication to work-life balance and freedom. This can lead to a more pleased and involved staff with lower turnover rates, lowering hire and training costs.

5. Filling Skill Gaps: Part-time jobs can be a strategic answer for addressing specific skill gaps within a company. Businesses can hire part-time experts to handle unique chores or projects without the commitment of a full-time role.

6. Enhanced Employer Branding: Organizations that offer part-time work choices are seen as innovative and flexible to different needs. This can draw top talent wanting freedom and work-life balance, boosting the company brand and attracting a bigger group of qualified applicants.

7. Greater Flexibility and Scalability: Part-time jobs allow companies to scale their staff up or down based on seasonal needs or project requirements. This offers greater agility and flexibility in a dynamic work setting.

While drawing a bigger range of talent is a major benefit, part-time work offers even more benefits for organizations:

1. Increased Innovation and Creativity: Part-time workers often bring fresh views and different experiences to the table. This can spark new ideas, question the status quo, and lead to innovative solutions within the company.

2. Improved Customer Service: Part-time schedules can allow for flexible hiring during busy hours or on weekends, ensuring excellent customer service when demand is high. This can lead to greater customer happiness and loyalty.

3. Reduced Risk and Increased Agility: Part-time jobs allow companies to test the waters with new projects or initiatives without a full-time commitment. This allows for controlled experimentation, lowers possible risks, and creates a more adaptable work atmosphere.

4. Improved Employee Morale: Offering part-time work choices shows an employer's knowledge of work-life balance and their commitment to employee

well-being. This can lead to a more positive and engaged staff.

5. Management Training Opportunities: Assigning supervisory jobs to manage part-time staff can provide useful training and development opportunities for full-time workers, honing their leadership and communication skills.

6. Enhanced Employer Branding: In today's competitive hiring market, giving part-time jobs shows an organization's commitment to freedom and work-life balance. This draws a bigger range of candidates, including those seeking job transitions, parents looking for re-entry chances, and individuals prioritizing well-being.

7. Improved Employee Engagement: Part-time workers often bring a burst of energy and new views due to their non-traditional schedules. This can energize the entire team and promote a more dynamic work setting.

8. Reduced Absenteeism and Turnover: Studies show that part-time workers may have lower absenteeism rates compared to full-time staff. Additionally, having part-time choices can help keep important talent who might otherwise leave due to inflexible schedules or childcare needs.

9. Knowledge Transfer and Succession Planning: Seasoned part-time workers, especially retired, can act as teachers to younger staff, promoting knowledge

transfer and ensuring stability of expertise within the organization. This is particularly useful in businesses with specialized skills or rapid technological advances.

10. Cost-Effective Training Opportunities: Part-time jobs can be used to train new hires or upskill current staff on specific tasks or projects. This allows for targeted training without the full expense of a full-time job.

11.Community Engagement and Social Responsibility: Part-time work can provide chances to partner with local organizations or educational institutions. This promotes a feeling of community involvement, strengthens the employer brand, and attracts people who value social duty.

For both people and organizations to reap the full benefits of part-time work, it's crucial to create clear standards, effective communication lines, and a supportive work atmosphere.
This includes:

Well-defined work descriptions and tasks

Transparent communication regarding plans, tasks, and goals

Opportunities for growth and improvement

Access to critical materials and tools
Recognition and thanks for efforts

By accepting part-time work as a strategic approach
to talent management and work style preferences,
both people and organizations can open a world of
possibilities, enabling a more flexible, productive, and
fulfilling work experience for all.

Chapter Three:

Overcoming Stigma and Misconceptions: Redefining the Value of Part-Time Work

In today's fast-paced world, the idea of work has grown beyond the standard picture of a full-time, nine-to-five commitment. Part-time work is increasingly becoming a viable and useful choice for people wanting flexibility, chasing personal goals, or balancing other responsibilties. However, despite its rising frequency, part-time work is often met with myths and stigma. This chapter tries to question these bad views and shed light on the real potential of part-time arrangements. We will address common stereotypes, debunk myths surrounding productivity and dedication, and equip you with strategies to fight stigma and push for part-time opportunities, eventually redefining the value of this diverse and dynamic work option.

1. Common Misconceptions and Stereotypes about Part-Time Work: Debunking the Myths

Part-time work, despite its growing fame, meets various misconceptions and stereotypes that can hold individuals back from pursuing or advocating for such chances. Here, we address some of the most popular lies and set the record straight:

Myth 1: Part-time work is only for students or retired.
Reality: Individuals from all walks of life choose part-time work for different reasons. Parents may seek freedom to handle babysitting and work, professionals might pursue further education or side hustles alongside their jobs, and people of all ages may have specific health limits or need to prioritize personal well-being. Part-time work is not limited to a particular demographic and can cater to diverse wants and goals.

Myth 2: Part-time employees are less dedicated or skilled than full-time workers.
Reality: Commitment and skill are individual traits, and not directly tied to the number of hours spent. Part-time workers often bring a strong work ethic and dedication to their jobs, leveraging their important time effectively. They may offer varied views and experiences, and their flexibility can be an asset to teams needing to adapt and react quickly.

Myth 3: Part-time work offers minimal job growth or development possibilities.
Reality: Part-time work can be a stepping stone to career growth, allowing people to gain useful experience, develop new skills, and build professional networks. It can also offer chances to test-drive different job paths or study specific areas of interest before committing to a full-time role. Additionally, some part-time positions offer training and development chances, adding to professional growth.

Myth 4: Part-time work offers poor financial security.
Reality: While full-time roles usually offer better income, some part-time jobs come with competitive salaries, perks, and even chances for overtime or commission-based earnings. Additionally, part-time work can greatly supplement income, allowing people to meet financial goals, handle student loans, or add to household finances.

Myth 5: Part-time work doesn't add directly to company success.
Reality: Part-time workers often play vital roles in various business functions, from customer service and office support to project-based tasks and specialized knowledge. Their efforts can be vital in keeping smooth processes, providing excellent customer service, and helping ongoing projects.
Additional Misconceptions and Stereotypes:

Myth 6: Part-time work is unstable due to frequent scheduling changes or absences.
Reality: While some part-time jobs might have fluctuating schedules, many offer stable and predictable schedules, meeting individual wants and preferences. Additionally, part-time workers often show high levels of reliability and dedication, valuing their work hours and tasks.

Myth 7: Part-time work lacks the sense of community or connection found in full-time jobs.
Reality: Building a feeling of community and belonging transcends the amount of hours spent.

Many companies actively promote inclusion and engagement for all workers, regardless of their work routine. Part-time workers can join in team events, build relationships with colleagues, and add to a positive work environment.

Myth 8: Part-time work is not "real work" and doesn't deserve career development chances.
Reality: All work gets attention and recognition, regardless of the number of hours devoted. Many companies give career development chances for all employees, including part-time workers. Investing in skill development empowers people to succeed in their jobs and add meaningfully to the company.

Myth 9: Part-time work is a dead end and doesn't offer chances for long-term job progression.
Reality: Part-time work can be a stepping stone to full-time chances within the same company or a gateway to exploring different job paths. By showcasing skills and commitment, part-time workers can place themselves for advancement or explore internal job openings as they arise.

Myth 10: Part-time work is only useful for the employer and not the individual.
Reality: Part-time work gives a win-win situation for both employers and workers. Employers gain access to skilled people, greater freedom, and reduced costs connected with full-time benefits. Employees gain important work experience, financial security, and the ability to balance work with other parts of life.

By debunking these beliefs, we can question the
stigma surrounding part-time work and recognize its
true value in creating diverse and adaptable
workforces, supporting individual needs and goals,
and adding to overall organizational success.

Beyond the specific myths and stereotypes stated, it's
important to recognize the complexity and nuances
regarding part-time work:

1. Not all part-time work is made equal:
Wages, perks, and job stability can vary greatly
across different businesses and even within the same
company. Some part-time jobs offer regular hours and
benefits, while others might be more temporary or
project-based with fewer benefits.

2. Individual experiences:
Each individual's experience with part-time work will
be unique, shaped by their special job, company
culture, and personal circumstances. While some
might face problems with scheduling or lack of perks,
others may find part-time work to be a highly
satisfying and empowering experience.

3. The changing environment of work:
The idea of "full-time" work is constantly evolving,
with many organizations accepting flexible work
arrangements and project-based contracts. This shift
emphasizes the worth of skills and talents over
standard definitions of "full-time" or "part-time" jobs.

4. Intersectionality and specific needs:
It's crucial to recognize the intersection of various factors that can influence an individual's choice to pursue or benefit from part-time work. Considerations like babysitting needs, disability accommodations, and financial limits all play a role in creating individual wants and experiences.

By knowing these additional aspects, we can move beyond a one-size-fits-all approach and recognize the varied and important contributions of part-time work in today's changing environment.

2. Debunking Myths Surrounding Productivity and Commitment in Part-Time Work:

The world of efficiency and dedication in part-time work is often shrouded in myths. Here, we dig deeper into debunking these myths and showing the truth behind the potential of part-time work:

Myth 1: Part-time workers are less productive than their full-time peers.
Reality: Studies have shown that part-time workers can be equally, if not more, effective than full-time employees. This can be linked to several factors:

Focus and efficiency: Working fewer hours can lead to improved focus and attention during work time. Part-time workers often have fewer distractions and are more likely to optimize their time for peak output.

Motivation and engagement: Knowing their time is limited, many part-time workers approach their work with increased motivation and engagement, trying to make the most of their given hours.

Reduced burnout: Working fewer hours can avoid burnout and tiredness, leading to sustained levels of energy and attention throughout the work time.

Myth 2: Part-time workers are less committed to their jobs and the company.
Reality: Commitment exceeds the amount of hours worked and is often tied to individual desire, purpose, and agreement with business values. Many part-time workers choose their specific jobs due to real interest in the work or a desire to gain specific skills and experience. Additionally, part-time workers often show high levels of loyalty to their companies, valuing the freedom and work-life balance offered by their schedules.

Myth 3: Part-time workers require more control and management.
Reality: Skilled and experienced part-time workers can often be highly independent and self-directed, needing minimal supervision once properly trained. Their familiarity with specific tasks and attention during work hours can add to their efficiency and ability to handle their workload freely.

Myth 4: Part-time work is unsuitable for complicated or demanding tasks.
Reality: Many projects are structured with specific outputs and dates that can be successfully completed within part-time schedules. Part-time workers with relevant skills and knowledge can be valuable assets to project teams, bringing a fresh viewpoint and focused effort to their given tasks.

Myth 5: Part-time work doesn't promote a strong team dynamic or feeling of belonging.
Reality: Building good team culture and a feeling of belonging is not contingent on the number of hours worked. Companies that actively support inclusion and interaction can create a strong sense of community, regardless of employees' work plans. Part-time employees can actively join in team meetings, collaborate on projects, and build important relationships with colleagues through various channels.

Myth 6: Part-time workers are not reliable and have higher absenteeism rates.
Reality: Studies often show no significant difference in absence rates between full-time and part-time workers. In fact, part-time workers, valuing their restricted work hours, may show increased reliability and dedication to their planned shifts. Additionally, flexible work arrangements, often linked with part-time jobs, can help people to handle personal appointments or unexpected situations without impacting their work responsibilities.

Myth 7: Part-time work hinders job growth and chances for advancement.
Reality: Part-time work can serve as a valuable stepping stone to job growth and advancement. It can provide chances to:

Gain valuable knowledge and skills in a specific area, making individuals more competitive for future full-time jobs. Demonstrate loyalty and work ethic to possible managers, even within the same company. Network with peers and supervisors, fostering relationships that can lead to future possibilities. Develop specific skill sets that cater to project-based work or independent possibilities.

Myth 8: Part-time work is not financially safe or reliable.
Reality: While full-time jobs usually offer higher base salaries, part-time work can still be financially secure and add greatly to an individual's income. This can be achieved through:

Competitive hourly pay and possibility for overtime or commission-based earnings. Reduced commuting costs and fees connected with full-time work. Supplemental income that can help to financial goals, debt management, or family income.

Myth 9: Part-time workers are not invested in the company's progress.
Reality: Part-time employees can be highly invested in the company's growth for different reasons:

Personal pride and happiness in their work and efforts. Desire to keep a positive working relationship and possibility for future possibilities. Alignment with the company's beliefs and goal, creating a feeling of purpose and ownership.

Myth 10: Part-time work is not a good choice for people wanting educational stimulation and challenging work.
Reality: Many part-time jobs offer intellectually stimulating and challenging work, based on the business and individual role. This can include:

Project-based work needs creativity, problem-solving skills, and independent thought. Specialized jobs in different areas demanding expertise and knowledge application. Opportunities to work on cutting-edge technologies or new projects, even within a limited period.

Myth 11: Part-time workers lack the necessary skills and experience for complicated jobs.
Reality: Generalizations about skills and experience based simply on work plans can be inaccurate. Many part-time workers hold extensive experience and skill in their various areas, making them valuable participants to complicated tasks. Their focused

approach and ability to plan can even lead to efficient completion of intricate projects within their given time.

Myth 12: Part-time employees are a burden on full-time peers, needing extra training and help.
Reality: When properly onboarded and integrated into the team, part-time workers can quickly become self-sufficient and helpful peers. Their fresh views and diverse skill sets can even benefit full-time team members, supporting teamwork and knowledge sharing.

Myth 13: Part-time work is unfit for leadership jobs or supervisory posts.
Reality: Leadership skills and the ability to effectively handle teams exceed the amount of hours worked. Part-time workers with strong leadership skills, clear communication, and effective sharing strategies can shine in managerial roles, adding to positive team relations and productive outcomes.

Myth 14: Part-time work hinders cooperation and teamwork.
Reality: With the rise of communication technology and collaborative tools, part-time workers can successfully participate in meetings, share ideas, and collaborate on projects regardless of their work location or schedule. Additionally, their varied views and experiences can enrich team discussions and lead to more creative and new solutions.

Myth 15: Part-time work leads to high employee loss rates due to lack of interest.

Reality: When given important work, chances for growth, and a sense of belonging, part-time employees can be just as engaged and committed as their full-time peers. Additionally, flexible work arrangements often linked with part-time jobs can lead to increased employee happiness and reduced turnover, eventually benefiting the company.

By understanding these falsehoods, we can recognize the potential for high output, strong commitment, efficient work styles, and useful contributions from part-time workers. As work models continue to change, knowing the realities surrounding part-time work is crucial for building a more inclusive and diverse work atmosphere that values and fosters the contributions of all people.

3. Strategies for Combating Stigma and Advocating for Part-Time Opportunities

Combating stigma and advocating for part-time work takes a multi-pronged approach, tackling the problem at individual, workplace, and societal levels. Here are key methods to consider:

Individual Strategies:

A. Owning Your Choice:
Choosing part-time work is a personal choice often driven by various reasons. When approaching possible

employers or navigating talks around your work plan,
owning your choice with confidence is crucial. Here's
how to do it effectively:

1. Be Clear About Your Reasons:
Start by being clear about your reasons for picking
part-time work. Some popular reasons include:

Balancing work and home commitments: This could
involve caring for children or elderly family members,
chasing educational goals, or managing health issues.

Exploring job options and gaining new skills: Part-time
work can be a stepping stone to explore different
fields, test-drive career tracks, and gain useful
experience while developing new skills.

Prioritizing well-being and personal fulfillment: Opting
for part-time work can enable a better work-life
balance, allowing you to explore hobbies, travel, or
commit time to personal growth.

2. Articulate the Value Proposition:
Once you've found your reasons, be prepared to
explain the value proposition of your choice.

Here's how:
Highlight the perks for you: Emphasize how part-time
work helps you to keep a healthy work-life balance,
achieve personal goals, and eventually contribute with
increased focus and energy during your work hours.

Frame it as a benefit for the employer: Explain how your flexible schedule can help the organization through reduced costs connected with full-time benefits, access to specific skill sets for specific project needs, or the ability to fill key roles during peak hours.

Focus on your commitment and contributions: Assure the boss that even with a part-time schedule, you are highly committed to your job and determined to achieve results and contribute meaningfully to the company.

By being clear about your reasons and easily expressing the value proposition of part-time work, you can dispel possible misconceptions and encourage a more open and useful conversation with potential employers. Remember, owning your choice and emphasizing the benefits both for you and the company can pave the way for a successful and satisfying part-time work experience.

B. Focus on Results and Contributions:
In the face of lingering stigma surrounding part-time work, one of the most powerful tactics is to show your value through real results and efforts. This involves constantly showcasing your productivity, commitment, and ability to perform within your assigned hours. Here's how to approach this effectively:

1. Exceed Expectations:
Set the bar high: Aim to regularly exceed standards in your given tasks and duties. Go the extra mile whenever possible, showing initiative and commitment beyond the bare minimum.
Track your achievements: Maintain a clear record of your achievements. This could include making targets consistently, exceeding sales quotas, resolving complicated problems, or creating innovative solutions.

Quantify your impact: Whenever possible, put your successes into measurable terms. This could involve quantifying cost savings, improved efficiency metrics, or good comments received from clients or coworkers.

2. Prioritize Efficiency and Time Management:
Optimize your work style: Be aware of your time and work quickly. Focus on providing high-quality work within your allocated hours, showing the value of your focused effort.

Communicate effectively: Maintain clear and open conversation with your friends and supervisor. Keep them informed about your progress, anticipate possible hurdles, and seek timely help when needed.

Be proactive and solution-oriented: Anticipate needs and aggressively give answers. This shows your initiative, problem-solving skills, and ability to add meaningfully within your allocated time.

3. Highlight Your Achievements:
Seek chances to share results: Look for suitable times
to share your success with your supervisor and peers.
This could involve short progress reports, team talks,
or private conversations.
Tailor your communication: Adapt your
communication style and amount of information to the
unique target.

Focus on the effect: When sharing your successes,
stress the positive impact your work has had on the
team, project, or company.

By constantly exceeding standards, showing
efficiency, and actively communicating your efforts,
you challenge the view of part-time workers as being
less effective or committed. You showcase your worth
and prepare the way for a more inclusive and
meritocratic work environment, where individual
efforts are recognized and valued regardless of work
schedules.

C. Challenge Assumptions:
Combating stigma surrounding part-time work
requires open conversation and facing
misunderstandings head-on. Here's how to "challenge
assumptions" as an individual strategy:

1. Identify the misconception: Pay attention to scenarios where you meet bad stereotypes about part-time work. This could be through direct statements, assumptions about your skills, or unequal treatment compared to full-time peers.

2. Choose your approach: Consider the circumstances and connection with the person holding the misconception. You can choose to participate in a private chat, raise the problem during a relevant discussion, or simply offer a brief clarification in the moment.

3. Respond respectfully:
Acknowledge their perspective: Begin by recognizing their point of view and avoiding conflict.

Provide accurate information: Share important information and data that challenge the stereotype. For instance, research studies showing the productivity of part-time workers, or highlighting the diverse reasons people choose this choice.

Share your personal narrative: If comfortable, quickly explain your own reasons for choosing part-time work and the value you bring in your job.

4. Encourage further dialogue:
Invite them to learn more: Encourage the person to learn more about the benefits of part-time work and its varied uses within various businesses and groups.

Offer additional resources: Share important study pieces, statistics, or business policies that support flexible work arrangements.

Remember:
Maintain a polite and professional tone throughout the talk.

Focus on facts and avoid getting angry or emotional. Aim to plant a seed of understanding and encourage further discussion.

By participating in respectful and fact-based conversation, you can question negative perceptions and contribute to a more inclusive and informed work atmosphere.

D. Network and Build Relationships:
Combating negativity surrounding part-time work requires building a network of individuals who share your values and goals. Here's how to "network and build relationships" as an individual strategy:

1. Seek out like-minded individuals:
Professional organizations: Join professional groups or online communities that support flexible work models and advocate for diverse work arrangements.

Training Programs: Seek training opportunities with people who value work-life balance and understand the challenges of part-time work.

Peer-to-peer Connections: Connect with peers or workers within your field who work part-time. Share stories and build a helpful network.

2. Advocate through your actions:

Be a role model: Showcase the positive aspects of part-time work by showing your output, dedication, and success within your assigned hours.

Share your experiences: Participate in talks and share your personal experiences with part-time work, showcasing its benefits and addressing common myths.

Offer help: Be a source of support and motivation for others considering or currently working part-time. Share tools, advice, and useful information.

3. Leverage your network:

Raise knowledge: Use your network to raise awareness about the value of part-time work. Engage in polite conversation with individuals who hold negative beliefs and share your positive perspective.

Promote flexible work options: Advocate for flexible work plans within your company by speaking with coworkers, managers, and decision-makers. Share tools and cases showing the benefits of diverse work styles.

Collaborate for change: Partner with your network to push for wider social change. This could involve backing efforts promoting work-life balance policies, pressing for flexible work regulations, or arguing for babysitting solutions that allow individuals to choose part-time work without losing their well-being or job goals.

By building a helpful network and actively sharing your positive experiences, you can contribute to dismantling the stigma surrounding part-time work and creating a more inclusive and flexible work environment for everyone.

E. Embrace Continuous Learning:
Choosing part-time work doesn't diminish the value of career growth. In fact, accepting continuous learning can be a powerful strategy to fight stigma and showcase your dedication and commitment, regardless of your work plan. Here's how:
1. Seek chances for growth:
Formal learning: Explore online classes, workshops, or licenses related to your job. Utilize your free time to improve your skills and information base.

Informal learning: Engage in self-directed learning through business publications, blogs, podcasts, or workshops.

On-the-job learning: Seek opportunities to learn new skills and broaden your knowledge within your present work. Volunteer for challenging jobs or shadow friends in different areas.

2. Cultivate a growth mindset:
Embrace challenges: View challenges and failures as chances to learn and grow.

Seek feedback: Actively seek constructive feedback from your boss or peers to find areas for growth.

enjoy learning: Acknowledge your growth and enjoy your learning successes, regardless of how small.
3. Showcase your learning:
Update your resume and LinkedIn profile: Highlight your newly gained skills and information.

Share your learning with colleagues: Offer to share your newly gained knowledge with your team through casual presentations or conversations.

Apply your learnings to your work: Demonstrate the value of your learning by bringing your new skills to your current projects and tasks.

Benefits of constant learning:
Enhance your skills and marketability: Remain competitive in the job market by keeping updated with industry trends and advancements.

Increase your value to your current employer: Demonstrate your commitment to professional progress and your desire to add effectively to the company.

Boost your confidence and self-efficacy: Feeling confident in your skills and knowledge can fight negative misconceptions about part-time workers and allow you to speak for yourself more effectively.

By accepting continuous learning, you send a strong message about your commitment to self-improvement and professional growth. This not only benefits your job growth but also helps dismantle the stereotype that part-time work equates to stagnation. It shows your dedication to excellence and places you as a valuable asset, regardless of your work routine.

Organizational Strategies:
Promote an open work culture: Foster a culture that values varied work styles and respects the accomplishments of all workers, regardless of their work plans.
Offer flexible work arrangements: Implement and promote various flexible work options such as part-time roles, job sharing, shortened workweeks, and online work opportunities.

Challenge internal biases: Train managers and leaders to spot and address unconscious bias against part-time workers.

Showcase success stories: Highlight positive cases of part-time workers who are successful and add directly to the company.

Rethink performance evaluations: Move beyond standard hour-based measures and focus on results, outcomes, and efforts to correctly assess the performance of all workers, including those working part-time.
Societal Strategies:
Raise knowledge about the perks of part-time work: Educate the public about the varied value offer of part-time work, addressing its economic, social, and individual benefits.
Challenge traditional work norms: Advocate for policies that support flexible work arrangements and remove outdated views of "full-time" as the only standard for worthwhile work.

Support policy changes: Lobby for and support policies that promote work-life balance, parental leave, and childcare choices, allowing people to choose part-time work without losing their well-being or job advancement.

Share personal stories: Individuals who thrive in part-time work experiences can share their stories to inspire others and question social stigma through personal narratives and recommendations.

Additionally:
Utilize facts and research: Use data and study results that highlight the benefits of part-time work and its positive effect on individual well-being, organizational success, and the general economy. Collaborate across sectors: Engage with business leaders, lawmakers,

and social groups to create a collaborative effort towards creating a more inclusive and flexible work environment that welcomes the full potential of part-time work.

By implementing these comprehensive strategies at various levels, we can dismantle the stigma surrounding part-time work and pave the way for a future where individuals have the freedom and flexibility to choose work arrangements that align with their personal needs and aspirations, ultimately contributing to a more diverse, productive, and fulfilling work environment for all.

Chapter Four:

Navigating the Part-Time Job Market

The part-time job market offers a diverse range of possibilities, catering to people wanting flexibility, supplementing their income, or getting useful experience. Whether you're a student, parent, or someone looking for a side hustle, this chapter provides you with the tools and strategies to manage this dynamic world.

Within these pages, you'll discover practical tips for uncovering interesting part-time chances, delve into promising sectors brimming with part-time jobs, and learn how to tailor your resume and interview skills for success in this unique work environment. So, take a deep breath, unleash your potential, and prepare to start on your trip into the exciting world of part-time work!

1. Practical Tips for Finding Part-Time Job Opportunities

Finding the right part-time job is like unearthing a secret gem – it takes a bit of exploration, resourcefulness, and smart planning. Here's a thorough guide to help you navigate the road towards securing the ideal part-time opportunity:

1. Self-Assessment – Know Thyself (and Availability)

1. Time Commitment:
Performing a full self-assessment regarding your availability is crucial before joining the part-time job market. Honesty is key in this step, as it will decide the type and scope of job you can realistically seek and avoid future conflicts and stress.

Here are some key things to consider when measuring your available time:

Weekly commitments: List down all your current commitments, including school plans, family tasks, extracurricular activities, and personal time needs (e.g., exercise, hobbies).

Time management skills: Be honest about your time management skills. If you fight to stick to a plan, consider starting with fewer hours or a flexible routine to avoid overwhelming yourself.

Energy levels: Consider your normal energy levels throughout the day. Some people function better working mornings, while others prefer afternoons or nights. Knowing your peak productivity times can help you target jobs that match with your energy patterns.

2. Skill Inventory:
Taking stock of your skills and experience is important for identifying suitable part-time job possibilities. This

goes beyond just official skills and certifications. Consider:

Hard skills: These are technical skills you've gained through school, training, or experience. Examples include computer literacy, software proficiency, foreign languages, or specific technical skills important to your job.

Soft skills: These are personal traits and interpersonal skills that add to your total effectiveness in the workplace. Examples include communication, teamwork, problem-solving, critical thought, time management, and planning.

Transferable skills: These are skills learned from past experiences (even volunteer work or hobbies) that can be applied to different job settings. Examples include customer service skills, leadership, flexibility, or public speaking.

3. Interests and Values:
Understanding your hobbies and ideals helps you align your work life with what truly means to you. This can greatly improve your job satisfaction and overall well-being. Ask yourself:

What kind of work setting do you thrive in? Do you prefer a fast-paced, dynamic workplace or a quieter, more organized ore? Do you enjoy working solo or collaboratively?

What are your hobbies and values? Are there specific fields or projects you're passionate about? Aligning your work with your values can lead to a more satisfying experience. For example, if you're passionate about environmental protection, you might seek chances with eco-friendly groups.

What job goals do you have? Even in a part-time role, consider how the job can add to your long-term work aspirations. Look for opportunities that help you to build useful skills and gain experience in your desired area.

By taking the time for complete self-assessment, you'll gain useful insights into your time constraints, strengths, and goals. This self-awareness will empower you to make informed choices as you start on your part-time job search and eventually find a position that aligns with your life and work goals.

2. Expanding Your Search Horizons: Unearthing Part-Time Opportunities Everywhere
Finding the right part-time job is like putting together a puzzle – the more diverse your search methods, the greater your chances of finding the perfect fit. Here's a closer look at the different paths you can explore to expand your job search horizons:

1. Online Job Boards:
These internet markets are a goldmine for part-time job seekers. Utilize known platforms like Indeed,

LinkedIn, and [job search engines unique to your area].

Maximizing your online search:
Refine your search: Utilize options like "part-time," "flexible hours," and terms related to your skills and hobbies. This helps cut down the search results and saves you important time.

Set up job alerts: Many platforms allow you to make customized job alerts based on your interests. This ensures you receive alerts whenever new job posts matching your criteria are posted.

Explore different categories: Don't limit yourself to specific job names. Browse larger categories relevant to your skillset and hobbies to discover possible possibilities you might have missed.

2. Company Websites:
Many businesses, especially bigger groups, keep specific career pages on their websites. These pages often show current job openings, including part-time roles.

Benefits of checking business websites:
Direct application: Often, you can apply directly through the company website, easing the application process.

Insights into company culture: Browsing the company website can provide useful insights into their work environment, values, and purpose, allowing you to assess if they match with your own.

Hidden opportunities: Not all part-time roles are listed on big job boards. Checking company websites can show hidden gems that haven't yet been widely spread.

3. Temporary and Staffing Agencies:
Partnering with respected temporary or staffing companies dealing in part-time jobs can be a smart move. These services connect job hunters with companies wanting temporary or seasonal workers in different areas.

Advantages of using staffing agencies:
Access to a wider network: Staffing agencies have built relationships with different companies, giving you access to a larger range of possible possibilities.

Expert guidance: Agencies often provide career advice and interview preparation assistance, increasing your chances of getting the job.

Variety of opportunities: They usually offer diverse part-time jobs across various fields, allowing you to explore different choices.

By actively exploring these different methods and combining them with your self-assessment, you'll be well on your way to discovering a varied range of part-time job opportunities that match with your needs, skills, and ambitions. Remember, the more proactive and clever you are in your search, the closer you get to finding the right part-time job that fits perfectly into your life.

3. Leverage Your Network: Turning Connections into Opportunities
The power of networking should never be underrated, especially when looking for a part-time job. Your network goes far beyond just your local circle of friends and family, and by tapping into it successfully, you can unlock a wealth of hidden possibilities.

1. Personal Connections:
Your current network is a useful asset. Start by reaching out to:

Friends and family: Share your job search goals with your close group. They might be aware of possible openings within their own jobs or through their personal connections.

Former coworkers and professors: Even if you haven't spoken to them in a while, reunite and tell them about your job search. They might have useful insights into related opportunities or be ready to refer you for jobs within their current business.

Mentors or career advisors: If you've had mentors or career advisors in the past, reach out and reunite. They can give guidance, share business insights, and possibly connect you with relevant professionals in their network.

2. Social Media:
Professional networking platforms like LinkedIn are powerful tools for growing your network and meeting with individuals in your preferred area. Here's how to leverage them effectively:

Build your profile: Create a thorough and engaging LinkedIn biography that shows your skills, experience, and job goals.

Join important groups: Participate in online groups linked to your area or business. This allows you to connect with like-minded individuals, engage in discussions, and possibly find job leads.

Engage with professionals: Actively meet with professionals in your chosen area. Reach out to people you find interesting, show your interest in their work, and ask thoughtful questions.

Follow related businesses: Follow companies you're interested in working for on LinkedIn. This helps you to stay updated on their job postings and network with their workers.

3. Community Resources:
Don't dismiss the power of your neighborhood
community:

Community centers and libraries: Many community
centers and libraries have bulletin boards where local
businesses promote job openings, including part-time
roles.

College campuses: If you're a student or new
graduate, check the career center or bulletin boards
at your college location. They often advertise
part-time jobs idea for students.

Local businesses: Visit local businesses you're
interested in working for and ask about possible job
openings. While they might not have posted jobs, a
personal approach can sometimes lead to unexpected
chances.

Remember, networking is about making real ties and
establishing yourself as a useful resource. By being
aggressive, engaging, and providing value to your
network, you'll increase your chances of discovering
secret job opportunities and getting the perfect
part-time position.

4. Tailor Your Application Materials: Making a First
Impression that Counts
In the tough world of job applications, standing out
from the crowd is important. This is where tailoring
your application materials – resume and cover letter –

becomes an essential step in showing your fit for the specific part-time job.

1. Targeted Resumes:
A generic resume might get your foot in the door, but a targeted resume especially created for each job application significantly increases your chances of getting an interview. Here's how:

Highlight relevant skills and experience: Carefully review the job description and identify the skills and experiences they describe as necessary. Highlight these unique skills and related events within your resume, using the same keywords and terms as the job description.

Measure your successes: Whenever possible, measure your achievements using numbers and data. This showcases the effect you've made in earlier jobs and provides tangible proof of your skills.

Adjust the language: Tailor the language of your resume to fit the tone and style of the company and the specific job description.

Keep it concise and relevant: While showing your skills and experience is important, avoid making a long document. Aim for a brief and well-formatted resume that is easy for the hiring manager to browse.

2. Cover Letter Power:
An engaging cover letter can be the deciding factor in getting an interview. Don't overlook its power! Here's how to create an effective cover letter:

describe yourself: Briefly describe yourself and show your interest in the specific job. Mention how you found out about the job opening.

Reiterate your qualifications: Briefly mention your essential skills and experience stated in the job description.

Express your excitement and value proposition: Explain why you are excited about the chance and highlight what you can bring to the team. Go beyond simply stating your skills and show how these skills can specifically benefit the company.

Keep it brief and compelling: Aim for a one-page cover letter that is clear, concise, and engaging. Proofread carefully before sending it.

By investing the time and effort to tailor your resume and cover letter for each unique job application, you demonstrate your genuine interest in the position and display your value offer to the company. This personalized method will make a strong first impact and increase your chances of landing that coveted part-time job.

5. Ace the Interview: Shining Through and Landing the Job

The interview is your chance to make a lasting impact and showcase your suitability for the part-time job. With the right planning and approach, you can easily step into the interview room and please the hiring manager.

1. Research is Key:
Demonstrate your real interest and effort by completing thorough research beforehand:

Company research: Learn about the company's purpose, beliefs, and goods or services. Visit their website and social media pages to gain insights into their work atmosphere and current news.

Position-specific research: Understand the exact responsibilities and needs of the advertised job. Familiarize yourself with the area and the team you'll be working with.

2. Practice Makes Perfect:
Preparation is key to beating interview nervousness and giving confident answers. Here are some ways to prepare:

Anticipate common questions: Research and practice your answers to common interview questions like "Tell me about yourself," "Why are you interested in this position?" and "What are your strengths and weaknesses?"

Prepare specific examples: Use the STAR method (Situation, Task, Action, Result) to organize your answers and provide clear examples of your skills and experience relevant to the job requirements.

Practice with a friend or family member: Conduct fake interviews to practice your answers, receive feedback on your communication style, and build confidence.

3. Be Enthusiastic and Professional:
First impressions count. Here are some tips to create a good and professional image:

Dress appropriately: Dress properly and dress yourself according to the company's work culture. Aim for an outfit that is clean, neat, and expresses confidence.

Arrive on time: Punctuality is important. Aim to arrive at the interview site 10-15 minutes early to show your respect for the hiring manager's time.

Maintain eye contact: Make eye contact with the speaker while speaking and listening. This shows confidence and attention.

Positive attitude: Be eager and show a positive attitude throughout the interview. Smile, show sincere interest in the talk, and ask thoughtful questions.

By showing your planning, enthusiasm, and professionalism, you'll stand out from the crowd and increase your chances of getting the part-time job. Remember, the interview is a two-way conversation. Be prepared to ask thoughtful questions about the company and the job to gain a better understanding of the fit between you and the chance. So, take a deep breath, showcase your strengths, and bravely step forward to ace your interview!

Bonus Tip: Be firm and patient. Finding the right part-time job might take some time and work. Don't get frustrated, keep trying, and stay focused on your goals. Remember, the right chance is waiting for you just around the corner!

By following these practical tips and putting in the committed effort, you'll be well on your way to getting the ideal part-time job that matches your skills, interests, and schedule.

2. Exploring Industries and Sectors with Part-Time Positions

The good news is that almost every industry offers some form of part-time work, making it easier than ever to find a job that fits your schedule and hobbies. Here's a breakdown of some important areas with ample part-time opportunities:

1. Retail and Customer Service:

Types of jobs: Cashiers, sales associates, customer service reps, baristas, food service workers.

Benefits: Often flexible hours, possibility for discounts, and chances to build interpersonal skills.
Drawbacks: Can be fast-paced and involve working evenings and weekends.

2. Healthcare and Social Services:

Types of jobs: Patient care helpers, administrative assistants, receptionists, exercise teachers, childcare workers.
Benefits: Rewarding work, chances to make a good difference, and potential for job advancement.
Drawbacks: May require specific training or licenses, and some jobs involve mental strain.

3. Administrative and Office Support:

Types of jobs: Data entry workers, receptionists, office assistants, virtual assistants, social media assistants.
Benefits: Opportunities to build planning and communication skills, and some jobs offer online work choices.
Drawbacks: Can be routine and require long hours sitting at a computer.

4. Education and Training:

Types of jobs: Tutors, teaching assistants, after-school program instructors, library helpers. Benefits: Rewarding work in shaping young brains, and possibility for flexible scheduling around school hours.

Drawbacks: May require specific skills and can involve working nights and weekends.

5. Hospitality and Tourism:

Types of jobs: Hotel cleaning staff, restaurant workers and bartenders, tour guides, event staff.
Benefits: Dynamic job atmosphere, chances to meet new people, and possibility for good tips.
Drawbacks: Can be physically hard, often involve odd hours, and may require working holidays.

6. Technology and IT:

Types of jobs: Web developers (part-time projects), freelance graphic artists, data analysts (part-time projects), content writers (freelance work).
Benefits: Often lucrative, offer possibility for remote work, and can help build skills in high-demand areas.
Drawbacks: Can be tough, require specific technical skills, and may involve solo work with self-discipline.

7. Creative and Media:

Types of jobs: Freelance writers, photographers, editors, social media managers, graphic artists (freelance gigs).
Benefits: Flexible schedule, work on projects you're excited about, and build a portfolio for future possibilities.

Drawbacks: Inconsistent work flow, income can be changeable, and needs strong self-marketing and business management skills.

8. Gig Economy and Freelance Platforms:

Types of jobs: Online teachers, virtual assistants, delivery drivers, pet sitters, house cleaners (through sites like Fiverr, Upwork, TaskRabbit).
Benefits: Maximum freedom, choose your own hours, and set your own rates.
Drawbacks: Income can be inconsistent, takes self-discipline and marketing skills, and may lack perks like health insurance.

9. Transportation and Logistics:

Types of jobs: Delivery drivers (car, bike, scooter), warehouse workers, dispatchers, transportation aides.
Benefits: Potential for good pay and tips, chances for outdoor exercise, and some jobs offer flexible schedules.
Drawbacks: Can be physically hard, involve long hours, and may require specific licenses or qualifications.

10. Non-Profit and Government:

Types of jobs: Administrative helpers, grant writers, community outreach directors, study workers.
Benefits: Rewarding work contributing to a cause you

believe in, chances to learn new skills, and possibility
for stable benefits.
Drawbacks: May come with lower pay compared to
private business, and jobs can be competitive.

11. Environmental and Sustainability:

Types of jobs: Park rangers, field researchers,
conservation helpers, eco-tourism guides, recycling
center workers.
Benefits: Rewarding work adding to environmental
protection, chances to work outdoors, and learn about
sustainability practices.
Drawbacks: Can be physically demanding, some jobs
involve irregular hours and rural areas, and may offer
lower pay.

12. Sales and Marketing:

Types of jobs: Sales associates (part-time
commission-based tasks), marketing assistants, social
media managers, event marketing assistants.
Benefits: Opportunities to improve conversation and
persuasion skills, possibility for good commissions,
and learn about different businesses.
Drawbacks: Can be performance-based and require
meeting sales goals, may involve travel and irregular
hours.

13. Personal and Professional Services:

Types of jobs: Personal trainers, fitness teachers, hair stylists, massage providers, dog walkers, house cleaners.
Benefits: Flexible schedule, work with people one-on-one, and utilize your skills and knowledge to help others.
Drawbacks: May recuire specific training or licenses, income can be variable, and require good marketing and business management skills.

14. Arts and Entertainment:

Types of jobs: Ushers, stage workers, music teachers, entertainers (part-time gigs), event staff.
Benefits: Dynamic and creative work atmosphere, chances to work in your field of love, and meet interesting people.
Drawbacks: Can be competitive, involve odd hours and travel, and income may be changeable.

15. Construction and Trades:

Types of jobs: Carpenters' helps, electricians' assistants, landscapers, painters' assistants, building workers.
Benefits: Potential for good pay, learn useful skills in a trade, and chances for physical exercise. Drawbacks: Can be physically demanding, involve working outdoors in all weather situations, and may require specific training or licenses.

16. Manufacturing and Production:

Types of jobs: Assembly line workers, quality control inspectors, machine users (with training), production helpers.
Perks: Potential for good pay and perks, chances to learn new skills and add to a product's creation.
Drawbacks: Can be repetitive and involve working in a fast-paced workplace, may require specific training or experience, and often involve shift work.

17. Agriculture and Farming:

Types of jobs: Farmhands, garden workers, farmers' helpers, animal managers (at farms or kennels).
Benefits: Opportunities to work outdoors, learn about gardening and animal care, and experience a different job setting.
Drawbacks: Can be physically demanding, involve working in all weather situations, and may require unique knowledge or experience.

18. Research and Academia:

Types of jobs: Research assistants, lab assistants, teaching assistants (part-time classes), teachers, library helpers.
Benefits: Opportunities to add to study projects, gain experience in a school setting, and learn new things.
Drawbacks: May require specific skills or experience, jobs can be tough, and pay for some roles may be lower.

By considering your hobbies, skills, and preferences, you can find a part-time job that not only fits your schedule but also helps you gain useful experience and add to your personal and professional goals.

Remember, exploring online job boards, company websites, and even networking with people in your desired field can help you discover even more hidden part-time possibilities. Don't be afraid to step outside your comfort zone and explore choices in areas you might not have initially considered. You might be shocked at the satisfying and rewarding part-time job waiting for you!

3. Resume and Interview Strategies Tailored for Part-Time Employment

Resume Strategies:
Highlight your flexibility: Clearly state your availability for part-time work in your resume brief or goal section. Specify if you have any desired work hours, days, or plans.

Focus on relevant skills and achievements: Even in a part-time job, you bring important skills and experience. Emphasize the most important skills and successes for the specific role, even if they come from previous part-time jobs, charity work, or academic projects.

Quantify your accomplishments: Use numbers and data whenever possible to showcase the effect you made in earlier roles. This shows your ability to give results, even with limited hours.

Tailor your resume for each job: Don't just send out a basic resume. Adapt your resume to show the specific skills and experiences stated in the job description.

Keep it simple and clear: Aim for a one-page resume for most part-time jobs. Use clear and concise wording throughout your resume.

Interview Strategies:
Express genuine enthusiasm: Even though it's a part-time job, show genuine interest in the chance and the company. Research the company and the job beforehand to show your knowledge and enthusiasm.

Be clear about your availability: Be upfront and transparent about your availability and any limits in your plan. Discuss your adaptability and desire to work around specific needs, if relevant.

Address possible concerns: Anticipate possible worries companies might have about hiring someone part-time, such as dependability or commitment. Be prepared to handle these issues by highlighting your strong work ethic, time management skills, and ability to organize tasks effectively.

Ask smart questions: Show your real interest in the company and the job by preparing intelligent questions about the position, the work environment, and the company culture.

Negotiate your compensation: Don't shy away from talking pay and perks, even for part-time jobs. Research average pay for related jobs in your area and be prepared to make a fair request.

Follow up after the interview: Send a thank-you email to the interviewer(s) within 24 hours of the interview, reiterating your interest in the job and your skills.

Additional Tips:
Network: Talk to friends, family, and past colleagues about possible part-time possibilities.

Utilize online resources: Many online sites and job boards specialize in part-time roles.

try freelance work: If you have special skills and experience, try freelance or contract work for more flexible schedules.

Be patient and persistent: Finding the right part-time job may take some time and effort. Be patient in your job search and don't get frustrated.

By focusing on these strategies, you can create an appealing resume and easily handle the interview process to increase your chances of getting the perfect part-time job that meets your needs and goals.

Chapter Five:

Making Part-Time Work Sustainable

While finding a part-time job can be a great way to achieve your desired work-life balance, it's crucial to understand how to handle the unique challenges associated with working limited hours. Beyond the original job search, ensuring the long-term longevity of your part-time work requires a smart approach to handling your funds, effectively juggling multiple jobs or gigs, and building a strong support network.
This chapter will serve as your complete guide to thriving in the world of part-time work. We'll dive into practical methods for:

Financial Management and Budgeting: Explore effective budgeting techniques and financial planning tips to ensure your part-time income can meet your wants and goals.

Balancing Multiple Jobs or Gigs: Learn how to effectively handle your time and workload when handling multiple part-time jobs or freelance gigs.

Building a Support Network and Accessing Resources: Discover how to build a network of like-minded people and find available tools especially designed to support part-time workers.

By mastering these crucial skills and utilizing the useful insights offered in this chapter, you can turn your part-time work into a sustainable and satisfying experience, paving the way for meeting your personal and professional goals.

1. Financial Management and Budgeting: Mastering Your Part-Time Income

Working part-time can offer amazing flexibility and freedom, but handling your finances on a changing income requires a different approach. This section will arm you with the essential tools and strategies to effectively handle your finances and ensure your part-time income allows you to meet your needs and achieve your goals.

1. Embrace Budgeting:
Budgeting, regardless of your income level, is essential to achieving financial well-being. It's the process of knowing your income and costs, then strategically allocating your resources to meet your wants and objectives. Here are three popular planning methods to consider:

1. 50/30/20 Rule: This widely used method offers an easy strategy for allocating your income:
50% for Needs: This covers necessary costs like rent, groceries, utilities, transportation, and minimum debt payments. These are non-negotiable costs important for your daily life.

30% for Wants: This area caters to your wishes and discretionary spending. It includes entertainment, eating out, sports, subscriptions, and non-essential items. Be aware of this area, as it directly impacts your ability to save and achieve financial goals.

20% for Savings and Debt Repayment: This important portion is committed to building your financial future. Allocate funds towards emergency savings, long-term goals like retirement or down payments, and quickly paying off high-interest debt.

2. Envelope System: This hands-on method is ideal for those who prefer a practical approach to handling their funds.
Here's how it works:

Categorize your spending: Identify your necessary and non-essential spending areas (e.g., food, transportation, activities).

Allocate cash: Withdraw a specific amount of cash for each buying area at the beginning of each pay period.

Track your spending: Use the given cash for each group and avoid exceeding the allocated amount. This method provides a visual picture of your spending and supports thoughtful buying habits.

3. Zero-Based Budgeting: This method gives a thorough approach to budgeting, ensuring every dollar has a set purpose.

Here's the process:

List all your income: Include your part-time salary, any other income sources, and projected income for the planning period.

List all your expenses: Categorize and list all your expected expenses, including set costs (rent, utilities) and variable costs (groceries, transportation).

Allocate your income: Assign each dollar of your income to a specific spending area, including savings and debt payback. This ensures every dollar is tracked for and stops unnecessary spending.

Choosing the most ideal budgeting method relies on your financial position, attitude, and tastes. Experiment with different methods to find one that connects with you and helps you effectively handle your part-time income. Remember, stability is key! By constantly tracking your costs and adhering to your chosen budget, you'll gain control over your finances and empower yourself to achieve your financial goals.

2. Prioritize Needs Over Wants:
While a part-time job offers freedom, it may also necessitate a change in spending habits. To ensure your income goes far enough, it's crucial to put needs over wants.

Here's how to tell between the two:

Needs: These are necessary expenses for your life
and well-being. They are non-negotiable and form the
basis of your financial security. Examples include:
Housing: Rent, mortgage payments, services
(electricity, water, gas).
Food: Groceries and necessary cooking materials.
Transportation: Public transportation prices, car
payments (if necessary for work or daily life), gas,
and basic car maintenance.
Healthcare: Medical bills, medications, and health
insurance payments.
Minimum debt payments: Avoiding late fees and
saving your credit score.

Wants: These are desirable things or events that
improve your lifestyle but are not essential for
survival. Examples include:
Dining out: Eating at restaurants, bars, or getting
takeout.
Entertainment: Movies, concerts, sports events,
subscriptions to streaming sites.
Non-essential shopping: New clothes, toys, tools, and
other discretionary purchases.
Travel: Vacations, weekend trips, and pleasure travel.

By prioritizing needs first, you ensure your basic
necessities are covered, promoting a sense of
protection and stability. Once your needs are met, you
can then allocate any leftover cash towards wants.
Making conscious choices:

Track your expenses: Analyze your buying habits to find places where you can cut back on wants.
Seek cost-effective alternatives: Explore cheaper substitutes for non-essential things, like cooking at home instead of eating out.
Embrace delayed gratification: Resist spontaneous buying and favor saving for future needs or wants.
Set realistic spending goals: Define your short- and long-term financial goals and match your spending decisions with them.

Remember, prioritizing needs over wants is not about deprivation; it's about making careful choices that fit with your financial goals and build a safe financial future. By taking this method, you strengthen your part-time income to meet your basic needs and prepare the way for achieving your goals in the long run.

3. Explore Additional Income Streams:
While a part-time job offers income, exploring additional income lines can greatly improve your financial security and accelerate your progress towards your goals. Here are some choices to consider:

1. Leverage your skills:
Freelancing work: If you hold special skills like writing, editing, graphic design, or programming, offer your services on freelancing platforms like Upwork or Fiverr.

Online teaching or tutoring: Share your knowledge and skills by tutoring online through sites like VIPKid or Chegg.

Virtual assistant services: Assist companies or people with routine chores, social media management, or email contact online.

2. Capitalize on the sharing economy:
Renting out empty space: Utilize platforms like Airbnb to rent out an extra room, parking space, or even storage space to create passive income.

Selling unused items: Declutter your things and sell them online through platforms like Jumia or Facebook Marketplace, or offline through yard sales.

3. Explore area opportunities:
Part-time gigs: Look for strange jobs or one-time gigs in your local area, such as dog walking, house-sitting, or participation in paid market research studies.

Seasonal work: Consider seasonal jobs during peak times, such as shopping during the holiday season or event help for festivals or concerts.

Remember:
Research and compare options: Explore different platforms, gigs, and online markets to find chances with competitive pay and fair working conditions.

Start small and grow up: Begin with one or two extra income streams to manage your time successfully and eventually grow as you gain experience and confidence.

Be aware of taxes: Understand your tax obligations and ensure you correctly report any extra income made.

By exploring these choices and utilizing your skills and resources, you can create additional income streams that support your part-time job. This extra income can help you cover your costs more comfortably, build your savings faster, and eventually achieve your financial goals with greater ease and speed.

4. Track Your Expenses:
Understanding where your money goes is important for making an effective budget. Utilize planning apps, spreadsheets, or even pen and paper to track your daily, weekly, or monthly costs. This helps find places where you can cut back and prioritize your spending.

5. Embrace Frugal Living:
Frugal living doesn't mean hardship; it's about making careful choices to improve your spending. Explore cost-saving alternatives like cooking at home, using public transportation, finding free entertainment choices, and shopping around for better deals on basics.

6. Automate Savings:
Set up regular payments from your checking account
to your savings account each payday. This "set it and
forget it" method guarantees consistent savings and
builds your financial safety net.

7. Plan for the Future:
Even with a part-time job, planning for your future is
important. Consider setting up a retirement plan,
even if it's a simple IRA, to leverage compound
interest in the long run.

8. Seek Financial advice:
Don't hesitate to seek professional advice from a
financial advisor who can help you build a
personalized financial plan and navigate your choices
based on your unique circumstances and goals.

By adopting these strategies and developing a careful
approach to handling your funds, you can empower
your part-time income to meet your wants and
ambitions, paving the way for a safe and fulfilling
future.

2. Balancing Multiple Part-Time Jobs or Gigs: Mastering the Juggling Act

Juggling multiple part-time jobs or gigs can offer
greater income, freedom, and different experiences.
However, successfully handling this workload requires
smart planning, effective time management, and a
dedication to keeping organized. Here's how to strike

a balance and succeed in this fast-paced
environment:

1. Prioritize and Schedule:
Effectively handling multiple part-time jobs or gigs
requires a well-defined plan that prioritizes your
responsibilities and ensures a healthy work-life
balance. Here's how to make a master plan and
organize your time effectively:

1. Create a Master Schedule:
List everything: Include all your work responsibilities
with information like start and end times, breaks, and
travel time.
Visualize your week: Utilize a physical planner,
calendar app, or online tool to make a visual picture
of your routine.
Color-coding: Consider using different colors to
differentiate between different jobs or tasks, making it
easier to scan and identify your duties.

2. Prioritize Wisely:
Identify important commitments: Analyze your work
obligations based on things like income, region, and
personal preferences.
Schedule first: Block out time for the most important
or time-sensitive tasks first in your plan.
Maintain flexibility: Leave room for unexpected events
or plan changes to avoid rigid limits.

3. Personal Time is Essential:
Block out non-work hours: Dedicate time for sleep, food, exercise, leisure activities, and social contact.
Maintain a healthy balance: Prioritizing personal time outside of work helps avoid burnout and supports overall well-being.
Schedule relaxation: Treat personal time seriously and plan it into your day to ensure you actively engage in activities that recharge and refresh you.

By making a thorough master schedule and prioritizing your responsibilities, you lay the basis for successfully juggling multiple jobs or gigs. Remember, this plan is your roadmap, so adapt it to your personal needs and don't fear to adjust it as circumstances change.

2. Optimize Your Time Management: Juggling multiple part-time jobs or gigs requires efficient time management skills. Here's how to utilize different techniques and tools to maximize your output and minimize stress:

1. Leverage Technology:
Embrace planner and to-do list apps: Utilize apps to plan tasks, set notes, and track your progress, ensuring you stay on top of goals and commitments across all your jobs.
Explore work apps: Consider apps like time trackers, project management tools, or focus timers to improve your organization and productivity further.

2. Batch Similar Tasks:
Group your activities: Instead of constantly moving between jobs, group similar activities together. For example, assign specific time blocks for returning emails, making phone calls, or running errands for all your jobs.
Minimize context switching: This repetitive process of moving between jobs can significantly hinder your output. Batching similar jobs reduces context switching and helps you keep focus and efficiency.

3. Utilize Downtime Strategically:
Don't waste short breaks: Instead of looking through social media, use breaks effectively. Catch up on emails, plan your next day's tasks, or simply relax your mind for a few minutes to keep energy levels throughout the day.
Plan for downtime: Schedule short breaks throughout your day to avoid stress and keep focus. You can even use these breaks for quick stretches, breathing routines, or light meditation.

Remember:
Experiment and find what works for you: Different people thrive with different tools and methods. Explore different choices and find a method that best fits your learning style and preferences.
Be realistic: Don't overload your plan or try to accomplish too much in a short period. Be realistic about your skills and schedule projects properly.

Delegate jobs when possible: If possible, consider assigning personal errands or jobs to free up more time for work and personal goals.

By applying these strategies and leveraging technology to your advantage, you can effectively manage your time, stay organized, and maximize your output even with multiple work responsibilities. This will help you achieve your goals and keep a good work-life balance.

3. Communication is Key: Fostering Open Dialogue and Collaboration
Maintaining openness and clear communication with your clients is crucial for successfully handling multiple part-time jobs or gigs. Here's how to create effective contact channels and navigate possible challenges:

1. Transparency from the Start:
Be upfront and honest: Inform each company about your other work responsibilities during the interview process or upon taking the job offer.
Maintain clear availability: Provide your companies with an exact and updated schedule showing your open working hours.
Foster trust and understanding: By being upfront about your position, you build trust and set the foundation for open conversation.

2. Negotiating Flexibility:
Discuss your needs: Explore the chance of flexible work plans with your bosses. This could involve fluid start and end times, shortened workweeks, or split shifts.
Highlight possible benefits: Explain how flexible plans could help the company, such as greater availability during peak hours or decreased need for extra hiring.
Be open to compromise: Be prepared to discuss and find a mutually beneficial solution that fits your needs and the employer's practical requirements.

3. Proactive Communication:
Anticipate conflicts: Identify potential schedule conflicts across your jobs and share them to your bosses as soon as possible.
Seek answers collaboratively: Work with your employers to find answers or alternative plans to limit disruptions and ensure timely completion of all your work responsibilities.
Maintain constant communication: Regularly update your managers on any changes to your plan or availability to avoid misunderstandings or missed chances.

Remember:
Effective conversation is a two-way street: Be receptive to your employers' comments and worries and carefully listen to their views.
Transparency promotes trust: Open communication builds trust and teamwork, making it easier to handle

unexpected obstacles and find solutions that benefit everyone.

Professionalism matters: Maintain a professional tone and demeanor in all your contacts, even when talking schedule changes or possible conflicts.

By following these communication strategies, you can create a good working relationship with your employers, ensure smooth collaboration, and effectively handle your multiple commitments while keeping professionalism and trust.

4. Stay Organized:

Managing multiple part-time jobs or gigs can easily lead to organizational mayhem. Here's how to create processes and utilize technology to keep clarity, minimize confusion, and maximize efficiency:

1. Create Dedicated Workspaces:

Physical separation: If possible, designate different physical workspaces for each job. This could be different rooms in your home, specific work booths in a co-working space, or even different parts of your desk.

Visual cues: Utilize visual cues like specific papers, folders, or computer screens dedicated to each job to enhance mental clarity and enable quick moving between tasks.

2. Organize Belongings:
Essential thing checklists: Create checklists of important things, paperwork, and tools needed for each job. This prevents last-minute scrambling and ensures you have everything easily available when needed.
Labeling and categorization: Label folders, files, and storage cases clearly to quickly identify and access job-specific information and materials.

3. Leverage Technology: Cloud storage: Utilize cloud storage services to store papers, files, and information available from any device, regardless of location. This removes the need to carry around physical copies and allows you to access information easily during your work shifts.
Project management tools: Explore project management apps to plan work, track progress, and share information across your different jobs. This creates a unified hub for all your work-related information and activities.

Remember:
Consistency is key: Maintain uniform organization practices across all your jobs to avoid misunderstanding and lost time looking for missing information.
Cleanliness is crucial: Regularly clean your workplace and digital files to avoid information overload and keep a clear and organized environment.
Find what works for you: Experiment with different organization systems and tools to discover a method

that best suits your learning style and working preferences.

By creating specific workspaces, organizing your things, and leveraging technology to your advantage, you can create a more organized and efficient work environment, minimizing the stress and anger of handling multiple responsibilities.

5. Prioritize Self-Care:
While handling multiple part-time jobs or gigs can be enriching and fulfilling, ignoring your well-being can lead to burnout anc hinder your productivity and overall satisfaction. Here's how to prioritize self-care and ensure your physical and mental well-being stay a top priority:

1. Schedule for Rest and Relaxation:
Block out downtime: Allocate designated time in your plan for breaks, rest, and sleep. This ensures you value your well-being and have sufficient time to recharge between work obligations.
Say "no" when needed: Don't be afraid to decline additional work chances or social events if you feel stressed or need time to rest. Prioritize your health and well-being to avoid stress.

2. Maintain Healthy Habits:
Fuel your body: Make mindful choices regarding your food intake. Prioritize healthy and nutritious meals to provide your body with the energy it needs to work at its best. Prioritize sleep: Aim for 7-8 hours of decent

sleep each night. Adequate sleep is important for keeping physical and mental health, attention, and brain performance. Move your body: Engage in regular physical exercise, even if it's just a brisk walk or a short yoga practice. Exercise helps handle stress, boosts energy levels, and improves general well-being.

3. Delegate When Possible:
Seek help: Don't be afraid to delegate personal jobs, chores, or home tasks to family members, friends, or even professional services. This frees up important time and mental room to focus on your work and well-being.

Utilize technology: Explore apps or services that can handle jobs like food delivery, online bill payments, or laundry pick-up and delivery. This can greatly lower your job and free up personal time.

Remember:
Self-care is not selfish: Prioritizing your well-being is not a luxury; it's important for keeping your energy, focus, and ability to handle your work and personal life successfully.

Listen to your body: Pay attention to your physical and mental needs. Take breaks when you feel tired, and schedule time for things you enjoy to keep a positive mental state.

Seek support: Don't hesitate to reach out to friends, family, or mental health professionals if you feel stressed or fighting to deal with the demands of your work and personal life.

By prioritizing self-care, incorporating healthy habits, and delegating chores when possible, you can ensure your well-being remains a top priority, enabling you to grow in your multiple endeavors and maintain a happy and sustainable work-life balance.

Remember:
Communicate and be transparent: Openly sharing your position with employers builds understanding and collaboration.
Prioritize your well-being: Taking care of yourself physically and mentally is important for sustaining your job and keeping long-term success.
Don't be afraid to adjust: As circumstances change or your needs grow, be flexible and adjust your plan or task to ensure a healthy balance.

By applying these practical tactics and valuing your well-being, you can effectively handle multiple part-time jobs or gigs, maximizing your income and work experience while keeping a healthy and satisfying lifestyle.

3. Building a Support Network and Accessing Resources for Part-Time Workers

Navigating the world of part-time work can come with its own set of difficulties. Building a strong support network and knowing where to find appropriate resources can greatly enhance your experience and general well-being. Here's how you can connect with others and receive useful information and assistance:

Building a Support Network:
1. Connect with colleagues: This creates a feeling of community and connection within the workplace. Sharing experiences and giving support can help navigate challenges and enjoy achievements together.

2. Join online communities: This opens doors to a bigger network of individuals having similar situations. Participating in online platforms and groups allows for exchanging useful information, sharing experiences, and getting different viewpoints.

3. Seek help from mentors: Mentorship provides essential advice and support from individuals with experience managing part-time work. They can offer insights into job growth, work-life balance, and overcoming unique challenges.

Here are some additional things to consider:
Be proactive: Take the initiative to meet with colleagues, join online groups, and seek out possible mentors.

Be open and receptive: Be willing to share your stories and constantly listen to others.

Give value: Contribute meaningfully to online groups and give help to others within your network.

Maintain connections: Nurturing relationships takes constant work. Stay in touch with peers, join in online discussions, and regularly check in with your mentor.

Building a strong support network can be incredibly helpful for part-time workers. By following these tactics and creating important relationships, you can gain valuable resources, handle challenges more effectively, and feel more powerful in your professional journey.

Accessing Resources:
This is a comprehensive list of tools that can be incredibly useful for part-time workers. Here's a breakdown of each item and its possible benefits:

1. Government Websites:
Information: Learn about your rights and laws regarding part-time work, including minimum wage, extra pay, and access to perks like sick leave.

Programs: Discover appropriate government programs that may offer financial assistance, training chances, or other support services for part-time workers.

2. Non-Profit Organizations:
Classes & Training: Gain important skills and information through classes or training programs especially designed for part-time workers. These programs can cover themes like time management, job growth, communication, or negotiation.
Career Counseling: Receive personalized advice and support from career advisers who understand the specific challenges and possibilities faced by part-time workers.

3. Labor Unions:
Advocacy: Unions fight for the rights and fair treatment of all workers, including part-time employees. They can help ensure you receive fair wages, perks, and working conditions.

Legal protection: In case of workplace disagreements, unions may give legal help or protection to protect your rights.

4. Educational Institutions:
Courses & Programs: Enroll in courses or programs that can equip you with useful skills related to your part-time work or future job goals. This could include learning new tools, building communication skills, or improving your financial knowledge.

Time Management: Gain insights and strategies for effective time management, a crucial skill for handling work, personal life, and any additional responsibilities you might have.

By discovering these tools, part-time workers can strengthen themselves with information, skills, and support to manage their work experience more effectively and achieve their job goals.

Additional Tips:
Those are all fantastic extra tips for part-time jobs! Let's break down why each one is valuable:

1. Network actively: This helps you:
Expand your professional network: Meeting people in your field can lead to new job possibilities, partnerships, or even mentorship opportunities.

Learn about possible opportunities: Staying connected within your industry can keep you informed about upcoming part-time jobs or independent work that might be a good fit for your skills and interests.

2. Advocate for yourself: Knowing your rights and being comfortable communicating with your boss is important for:

Ensuring fair treatment: Understanding your rights regarding things like schedules, breaks, and perks helps ensure you're treated fairly and receive what you're allowed to as a part-time worker.

Addressing issues: If you have any concerns about your work situation, don't hesitate to share them to your boss in a professional and respectful way.

3. Stay informed: Keeping up-to-date information is helpful because:

Industry trends: Staying updated about trends in your field can help you spot new skills you might want to learn to stay competitive and current.

Rules: Being aware of any changes in rules or laws regarding part-time work ensures you're legal and protects your rights.

New resources: New resources and programs especially for part-time workers might become available, and staying informed helps you take advantage of them.

By incorporating these extra tips along with the strategies for building a support network and accessing resources, part-time workers can set themselves up for success in their career journeys.

By actively building a support network and utilizing available resources, you can place yourself for success in the world of part-time work. Remember, you are not alone, and there are numerous tools available to ensure your part-time work experience is positive and adds to your total job goals and personal fulfillment.

Chapter Six:

Thriving in a Part-Time Career

In today's broad workforce, the part-time job path is a growing choice for many. While often seen as a stepping stone or temporary answer, a part-time job can actually be a rewarding and enriching experience, giving flexibility, balance, and even personal growth. This chapter dives into the world of thriving in a part-time job, leading you through the process of cultivating meaning and purpose in your work, even with reduced hours. We'll explore strategies for setting goals aligned with your personal values, ensuring your part-time activities add not just to your financial well-being, but also to your general sense of fulfillment. Additionally, we'll tackle the crucial aspect of self-care, giving practical tips to prevent burnout and maintain a healthy work-life balance, even amidst a possibly demanding schedule. So, whether you're a student, parent, caregiver, or simply wanting a more flexible work life, this chapter is your guide to thriving in a part-time job.

1. Thriving in a Part-Time Career: Cultivating Meaning, Balance, and Growth

While often viewed as a temporary situation, a part-time job can be a smart choice offering a unique mix of freedom, work-life balance, and personal growth. This chapter delves into the secrets of thriving in a part-time job, helping you develop meaning and purpose even with limited hours.

1. Cultivating Meaning and Purpose:
Many of us approach work as a means to an end, a way to pay the bills and achieve financial security. However, in a part-time job, where hours are limited, it becomes even more crucial to discover the deeper "why" behind your work. This "why" is the driving force that changes your part-time job from a mere duty to a source of meaning and personal satisfaction.

1. Delving into Your Values:
Self-reflection: Dedicate time to thought. Consider questions like: What values are most important to me? What kind of effect do I want to make in the world? What are my special skills and talents that I can offer? Journaling, taking personality assessments, or participating in guided meditations can be useful tools in this process.

Identifying hobbies: Explore your hobbies and interests. What hobbies bring you joy and a sense of satisfaction outside of work? Can you spot any connections between your hobbies and possible part-time roles? Perhaps you're passionate about environmental sustainability, and taking a part-time job with a local eco-friendly group could align with your values and interests.

2. Aligning Work with Your "Why":
Once you have a better idea of your "why," you can actively seek opportunities that resonate with you.

Researching Values-Driven Organizations: Many organizations have clearly stated mission statements and core values easily available on their websites or social media pages. Look for companies whose values match with your own, even if they aren't directly stated. Researching a company's mindset and employee reviews can also offer useful information.

Tailoring Your Job Search: Modify your resume and cover letter to show your values and how they connect with the particular company and job you're applying for. During interviews, use the chance to ask questions about the company culture and purpose, showing your genuine interest in aligning your work with your personal values.

3. Reframing Your Perspective:
It's easy to fall into the trap of feeling inadequate or less important due to a part-time plan. However, it's vital to shift your attention from the amount of hours spent to the quality and impact of your contribution.

Excellence, not Quantity: Strive for ease and success in your work. Focus on providing high-quality results that meet or exceed expectations, even within the shorter time frame of your part-time job. This shows your dedication and value to the company, regardless of the number of hours worked.

Identifying Metrics of Success: Establish clear metrics for success within your job. Instead of focusing solely on the number of hours spent working, outline measurable outcomes that show your positive effect. This could involve beating sales goals, streamlining processes, or creating successful marketing campaigns within your set time frame.

4. Embracing Continuous Learning:
Learning doesn't stop after college or official education. A part-time job gives a unique chance to continuously learn and build new skills.

Finding Growth Chances: Be proactive in finding chances for learning within your part-time job. This could involve volunteering for new projects, requesting mentorship from older workers, or attending training sessions given by the company.

Exploring External Resources: Utilize online courses, workshops, or conferences connected to your job to stay up-to-date with industry trends and acquire new skill sets. Investing in your own learning displays initiative and a dedication to personal and professional growth, enhancing your worth both within your present job and in future career pursuits.

By unearthing your "why," aligning your work with your values, reframing your view on contribution, and accepting continuous learning, you can develop a sense of meaning and purpose in your part-time job. Remember, thriving in a part-time job is not about working the most hours, but about working with purpose and a deep understanding of what motivates and fulfills you.

2. Setting Goals and Managing Priorities:
In a world of limited hours, setting clear goals and handling tasks effectively become important skills for thriving in a part-time job. By creating a plan for your aims and adopting strategies for optimal time management, you can ensure that your part-time activities add meaningfully to your overall goals while keeping a healthy work-life balance.

1. Setting SMART Goals:
SMART goals provide a structured framework for setting clear, realistic, and measurable targets. Applying this strategy to your part-time job helps ensure that your efforts are directed towards achieving important results, even within a limited timeframe.

Specific: Clearly describe your desired result. Instead of a general goal like "improve my skills," try something specific like "complete a certification course in X by Y date."

Measurable: Establish clear standards to measure your growth. This could involve quantifiable measures like finishing a specific amount of modules or getting a certain score on an exam.

Attainable: Set goals that are practical and achievable within the constraints of your part-time plan and present resources. Setting highly ambitious goals can lead to despair and hinder your progress.

Relevant: Ensure your goals align with your "why" and add to your wider job aspirations. Link your part-time goals to your long-term vision, ensuring they add to your overall professional growth.

Time-bound: Define a specific period for achieving your goals. This provides a sense of urgency and helps you stay on track. Consider breaking down bigger goals into smaller, more manageable steps with achievable dates.

2. Mastering the Art of Time Management:
With limited hours, optimizing your time management skills becomes crucial for combining your part-time work with other tasks and personal commitments. Here are some useful methods to consider:

Creating a Daily plan: Develop a daily plan that describes your work tasks, personal obligations, and specific time for rest and relaxation. Utilize tools like calendars, planners, or time management apps to picture your routine and track your progress.

Prioritizing jobs: Not all jobs carry the same weight. Employ prioritization techniques like the Eisenhower Matrix to identify pressing and important tasks, assign or schedule less crucial activities, and remove useless time-wasters.

Setting sensible goals: Be sensible when setting goals for yourself. Factor in unplanned delays and buffer time into your routine to avoid feeling overloaded and worried.

Leveraging Technology: Utilize various tools and technologies to improve your process. Consider using time trackers to measure your activity, apps like noise-canceling headphones to improve focus, or project management software to plan tasks and work with peers.

3. Maintaining a Healthy Work-Life Balance:
While prioritizing your career goals is important, keeping a good work-life balance is equally vital. Ignoring your personal needs can lead to burnout, impacting your general well-being and hindering your success in both job and home life.

Scheduling Personal Time: Block out dedicated time in your plan for activities that add to your well-being, such as exercise, hobbies, spending time with loved ones, or practicing relaxation methods.

Setting limits: Establish clear limits between your work and home life. This could involve communicating your working hours to coworkers and bosses and politely declining requests that fall outside your agreed-upon commitment.

Learning to Say No: Don't overload your schedule with unnecessary obligations. Be comfortable saying no to extra tasks or responsibilities that would compromise your well-being and ability to keep a good work-life balance.

By setting SMART goals, adopting effective time management strategies, and prioritizing your well-being, you can handle the demands of a part-time job while fostering personal and professional growth. Remember, thriving in a part-time job requires a holistic approach, balancing your work goals with your need for rest, relaxation, and personal satisfaction.

3. Strategies for Self-Care and Avoiding Burnout:
While a part-time job offers flexibility and possible work-life balance, it's still important to prioritize self-care and prevention of burnout to avoid jeopardizing your well-being and performance. Here are some important tactics to consider:

1. Knowing Your Limits:
Self-Awareness: The first step in protecting yourself from burnout is honest self-awareness. Recognize your individual limits in terms of task, stress tolerance, and time available. Don't be afraid to say no to extra responsibilities or requests that exceed your ability.

Open Communication: Communicate freely with your boss about your limits and desired work-life balance. Discuss your plan, task goals, and any worries you might have. A supportive boss will work with you to find a sustainable solution.

2. Nurturing Your Well-Being:
Prioritizing Self-Care: Schedule things that support your physical and mental well-being. This could involve:

Physical activities: Regular exercise helps handle stress, boost energy levels, and improve attention.

Healthy eating: Balanced and healthy meals provide your body with the fuel it needs to work optimally.

Mindfulness practices: Activities like meditation or yoga can help control stress, improve sleep quality, and increase general well-being.

Connecting with loved ones: Prioritize time for friends and family. Social connections provide important support and add to feelings of belonging and happiness.

Creating a Relaxing Routine: Establish a relaxing routine before and after work to help you move between your business and personal life. This could involve reading, taking a bath, listening to calming music, or spending time in nature.

3. Setting and Communicating Boundaries:
Establishing Clear limits: Define clear limits regarding your work hours, flexibility, and tasks. Communicate these limits clearly to your friends and employer.

Saying No Assertively: Be comfortable and bold in declining requests that fall outside your agreed-upon commitment or would compromise your well-being. Explain your reasons politely and avoid feeling obligated to accept additional workload if it doesn't match with your set limits.

Respecting Others' Boundaries: While setting your boundaries is important, also respect the boundaries of your coworkers and employer. Avoid making ridiculous demands or requests that could disrupt their work-life balance.

4. Seeking Support and Maintaining Perspective:
Building a Support Network: Don't hesitate to seek support from coworkers, teachers, or even professional psychologists if you're facing difficulties or feeling stressed. Talking to someone you trust can provide valuable advice, help you manage stress, and keep a healthy viewpoint.

Recognizing Warning Signs: Be aware of the warning signs of burnout such as constant tiredness, cynicism, reduced output, and social withdrawal. If you experience any of these symptoms, it's crucial to address them quickly through self-care practices, getting professional help if necessary, and possibly adjusting your workload or plan.

By prioritizing self-care, setting and communicating limits, and building a helpful network, you can successfully combat burnout and handle the challenges of a part-time job. Remember, your well-being is important, and a healthy work-life balance is essential for thriving in any professional setting.

Thriving in a part-time job isn't just about working fewer hours; it's about working better and with purpose. By focusing on finding meaning, setting clear goals, and valuing self-care, you can create a rewarding and enriching work experience, even with limited hours. Remember, your part-time job can be a moving stone, a source of personal growth, or simply a way to achieve a desired work-life balance. Embrace the unique possibilities it offers and use this chapter as a guide to navigate your road towards thriving in a part-time world.

2. Setting Goals and Aligning Work with Personal Values:

In a job world increasingly accepting flexible work arrangements, the part-time role has become a viable and even strategic choice for many. However, the thought of working fewer hours can sometimes lead to a feeling of diminished meaning or satisfaction.

This is where the strong mix of goal setting and aligning work with personal values comes into play.

The foundation of important work, regardless of the amount of hours worked, lies in knowing your "why". This "why" is your personal north star, the driving principle that drives your purpose and pushes you beyond just the paycheck. To reveal your "why," start on a journey of self-discovery:

Self-Reflection: Dedicate time to reflection. Ask yourself things like:

What are my core values?
What values are most important to me? (Integrity, creativity, helping others, natural survival etc.)
What effect do I want to make in the world? What kind of memory do I want to leave behind?
What are my skills and talents?
What do I enjoy doing?

Value Exploration: Explore your hobbies and interests. What hobbies bring you joy and a sense of satisfaction outside of work?
Can you spot any connections between your hobbies and possible part-time roles?

Tools for Self-Discovery:
Journaling: Regularly writing down your thoughts and feelings can help you gain focus and spot recurring themes and values.

Personality assessments: Online or professional personality exams can prov de insights into your skills, interests, and beliefs.

Guided meditations: Meditation techniques can help you quiet your mind and connect with your inner voice, leading to greater se f-awareness.

Once you have a clearer idea of your "why," you can actively seek out chances that resonate with you.

Researching Values-Driven Organizations: Many organizations have clearly stated mission statements and core values easily available on their websites or social media pages. Look for companies whose values match with your own, even if they aren't directly stated. Researching a company's culture and employee reviews through online sites like Glassdoor can also offer useful insights.

Tailoring Your Job Search: Modify your resume and cover letter to show your values and how they connect with the particular company and job you're applying for. During interviews, use the chance to ask questions about the company culture and purpose, showing your genuine interest in aligning your work with your personal values.

Beyond Alignment: Going the Extra Mile
Finding a part-time job that aligns with your values is a great first step; however, you can further improve your sense of meaning and satisfaction by:

Seeking Opportunities for Growth: Look for ways to add your unique skills and talents to projects or efforts that connect with your ideals. Volunteering for tasks outside your core responsibilities can show your heart and commitment to the organization's goal.

Building Meaningful Relationships: Connect with coworkers who share similar values and hobbies. Foster a sense of community within your workplace, building a support system that strengthens your sense of purpose and belonging.

Advocating for Change: If the organization's practices or policies contradict your values, consider ways to advocate for positive change in a polite and helpful manner.

Setting SMART Goals: Aligning Your Efforts with Your Aspirations

Now that you have a better understanding of your "why" and how it fits with your work, it's crucial to set SMART goals to guide your efforts and track your progress. SMART goals are:

Specific: Clearly describe what you want to achieve. Instead of a general goal like "improve my skills," try something specific like "complete a certification course in X by Y date."
Measurable: Establish clear standards to measure your growth. This could involve quantifiable measures

like finishing a specific amount of modules or getting
a certain score on an exam.
Attainable: Set goals that are practical and achievable
within the constraints of your part-time plan and
present resources. Setting highly ambitious goals can
lead to despair and hinder your progress.
Relevant: Ensure your goals align with your "why" and
add to your wider job aspirations. Link your part-time
goals to your long-term vision, ensuring they add to
your overall professional growth.
Time-bound: Define a specific period for achieving
your goals. This provides a sense of urgency and
helps you stay on track. Consider breaking down
bigger goals into smaller, more manageable steps with
achievable dates.

Examples of SMART Goals in a Part-Time Role:

Aligned with Personal Values:
Environmental Sustainability: If environmental
sustainability is a core value, a SMART goal could be:
"Volunteer for 2 hours per month with a local
environmental organization to participate in clean-up
initiatives by [date]."

Social Impact: If contributing to social good is
important, a goal might be: "Dedicate 1 hour per
week to researching and implementing a new
recycling program in my part-time workplace by
[date]."

Imagination: If unleashing your imagination is a value, a goal could be: "Complete an online course on graphic design and use the acquired skills to redesign the company's social media graphics by [date]."

Professional Development:
Skill Development: "Complete the online course 'X' offered by [platform] to learn [specific skill] by [date] and incorporate the new skill into my work by [date]."

Networking: "Attend 2 industry networking events by [date] to connect with 5 professionals in my field and expand my professional network."

Career Exploration: "Conduct informational interviews with 3 individuals working in my desired full-time career path by [date] to gain insights and explore potential career transition opportunities."

Performance and Efficiency:
Productivity: "Increase my typing speed by 10 words per minute by completing an online typing course and practicing for 30 minutes daily by [date]."

Customer Satisfaction: "Achieve a customer satisfaction rating of 90% or above on all customer interactions within the next quarter by actively implementing communication best practices."

Project Management: "Complete all assigned tasks for Project X on time and within budget by [date] by utilizing effective time management techniques and collaborating efficiently with team members."

These are just a few examples, and the options for SMART goals within a part-time job are vast. Remember, the key is to tailor your goals to your specific "why," ensure they are SMART, and use them as a roadmap to navigate your journey towards a happy and useful part-time job experience.

3. Strategies for Self-Care and Avoiding Burnout in a Part-Time Role

While a part-time job offers flexibility and possibly reduced work hours, it's still crucial to value self-care and burnout prevention. The demanding nature of handling work, personal life, and other tasks can quickly deplete your energy and lead to feelings of stress, exhaustion, and eventually, burnout. Here are some comprehensive strategies to develop resilience and avoid burnout in a part-time role:

1. Setting Boundaries and Prioritizing Well-being: Establish Clear limits: Define clear limits between your work and home life. Communicate your working hours, availability, and limits directly to your coworkers and employer. This includes:

Sticking to your agreed-upon schedule: Avoid the temptation to work beyond your planned hours unless totally necessary.

Learning to say no: Don't be afraid to politely decline additional work requests that would compromise your well-being or exceed your agreed-upon task.

Disconnecting after work: Avoid checking work emails or replying to work messages outside of your work hours.

Prioritize Self-Care: Schedule things that feed your physical and mental well-being into your routine:

Physical activity: Regular exercise helps handle stress, boosts energy levels, and improves sleep quality. Aim for at least 30 minutes of moderate-intensity exercise most days of the week.

Healthy diet: Eating balanced and nutritious meals provides your body with the fuel it needs to work properly.

Mindfulness practices: Activities like meditation, yoga, or deep breathing exercises can help handle stress, improve focus, and increase general well-being.

Relaxation techniques: Find healthy ways to rest and de-stress, such as spending time in nature, reading, listening to quiet music, or taking a relaxing bath.

Prioritize sleep: Aim for 7-8 hours of great sleep each night to help your body and mind to recover.

2. Cultivating a Supportive Network:
Connect with Loved Ones: Nurture your social relationships with friends, family, and loved ones. Spending time with people who support and care for you can provide a sense of belonging, reduce stress, and improve your happiness.

Seek Guidance: Don't hesitate to seek support from peers, teachers, or even professional counselors if you're facing challenges or feeling stressed. Talking to someone you trust can provide valuable advice, help you manage stress, and keep a healthy viewpoint.

3. Recognizing Warning Signs and Taking Action:
Be Aware of the Signs: Be familiar with the warning signs of burnout so you can spot them early on. These can include:

Constant fatigue: Feeling tired even after getting enough sleep.

Increased cynicism and negativity: Feeling distant and cynical towards your work or peers.

Reduced productivity: Difficulty concentrating and finishing chores quickly.

Changes in hunger or sleep patterns: Experiencing major changes in eating habits or sleep quality.

Withdrawal from social activities: Losing interest in things you used to enjoy.

Taking Action: If you experience any of these warning signs, it's crucial to take action to avoid further stress. This could involve:

Reducing your workload: Talk to your boss about changing your work hours or tasks if possible.

Taking a break or vacation: Even a short break from work can help you recover and return feeling refreshed and inspired.

Seeking professional help: Consider talking to a therapist or counselor who can provide advice and support on handling stress and avoiding burnout.

4. Maintaining a Positive Mindset:
Practice Gratitude: Taking time to enjoy the positive parts of your life, even the small things, can create a feeling of positivity and well-being.

Focus on Progress, not Perfection: Don't be overly critical of yourself or aim for impossible perfection. Instead, focus on celebrating your growth and successes, big or small.

question Negative Thoughts: Identify and question negative thought patterns that may be adding to stress and burnout.

Maintain a Growth Mindset: Believe in your ability to learn and grow from your experiences, even failures.

By prioritizing self-care, setting healthy limits, cultivating a supportive network, and keeping a positive attitude, you can successfully combat burnout and handle the challenges of a part-time job. Remember, self-care is not a luxury but a requirement for thriving in any work setting, regardless of the number of hours you work.

Chapter Seven:

The Future of Work

The landscape of work is facing a seismic change. Driven by a confluence of technological breakthroughs, demographic changes, and changing societal needs, standard ideas of work are being reshaped. This chapter looks into the exciting yet uncertain future of work, shedding light on the expected trends that will shape the workforce and work arrangements.

We will explore the necessity of accepting flexibility and adaptability in a rapidly changing job market, equipping ourselves to thrive amidst constant change. Furthermore, we will explore the possibilities and challenges provided by technological advancements and automation, looking to understand how we can leverage technology's potential while mitigating its disruptive effects. As we manage this shifting environment, this chapter aims to equip you with the information and insights necessary to not only live but also succeed in the future of work.

1. Predictions and Insights: Reshaping the Workforce and Work Arrangements

The future of work offers a dynamic and possibly disturbing change of the workforce and work arrangements. While the exact details remain hazy, various guesses and insights offer valuable views into this changing landscape:

1. Rise of Automation and AI: Technological developments, especially in automation and artificial intelligence (AI), are expected to greatly affect the workforce. While some jobs will be displaced, new possibilities will appear needing skills in areas like AI management, data analysis, and human-machine collaboration.

2. Skill Evolution and Upskilling: The rapid pace of technological change requires an ongoing dedication to skill evolution and upskilling. Individuals will need to continuously develop new skills and change current ones to stay relevant in the changing job market.

3. The Gig Economy and Flexible Work: The standard 9-to-5 job structure may become less common, with a rise in independent and contract work forming the "gig economy." This trend, alongside technological developments, allows for greater freedom in work arrangèments, offering both opportunities and challenges for workers and companies alike.

4. Globalized Workforce: Technological improvements and online work possibilities are leading to a more globalized workforce, with people working across countries and cultures. This presents possibilities for teamwork and varied views but also raises questions about cultural sensitivity, communication, and legal frameworks.

5. Focus on Soft Skills: While technical skills remain important, the future of work is likely to put a premium on "soft skills" such as critical thought, imagination, problem-solving, communication, and teamwork. These skills are vital for managing complicated settings, collaborating successfully, and adapting to change.

6. Importance of ongoing Learning: With the steady development of work, ongoing learning will become increasingly important. Individuals will need to be self-directed learners, constantly seeking out new knowledge and skills to stay competitive and flexible.

7. Automation and AI Specialization: While automation may replace some jobs, it will also create new roles focused on controlling and working with AI. These jobs will require expertise in specific areas like AI ethics, data security, and human-centered design.

8. The Rise of the "Hybrid" Workplace: The future is likely to see a mix model b ending online and in-person work arrangements. This offers freedom and improved output but also requires robust communication, collaboration tools, and strategies to promote a cohesive work culture despite physical distance.

9. The Evolving Role of Education: Educational institutions will need to change to prepare pupils with the skills needed for the future of work. This may involve incorporating real-world uses, developing

critical thought, and supporting adaptability and lifelong learning.

10. Focus on Well-being and Mental Health: The increasingly challenging and lively work environment will necessitate a stronger focus on employee well-being and mental health. Organizations will need to value work-life balance, adopt mental health tools, and create a supportive work atmosphere.

11. The Rise of the "Human-Plus" Era: With AI and technology taking over routine tasks, human workers will increasingly focus on tasks that leverage specifically human skills like creativity, empathy, and problem-solving. This will require a shift in mindset and a focus on building these "human-plus" skills.

12. The Evolving Nature of Work-Life Integration: As work becomes more fluid and technology breaks the lines between work and personal life, we need to create methods for good work-life integration. This might involve setting limits, utilizing technology effectively, and valuing personal well-being.

These are just a few of the predictions and ideas affecting the future of work. By knowing these trends and preparing for them, people and groups can better manage the changing environment and seize the opportunities that lie ahead.

Further Considerations: Nuances and Challenges in the Future of Work

While the previous parts highlight several trends and predictions, it's important to recognize the nuances and challenges that follow the future of work:

1. The Uneven Pace of Change: The effect of these trends will likely be uneven across different businesses, geographic areas, and socioeconomic groups. This can worsen current inequalities and require tailored solutions to ensure inclusive involvement in the future of work.

2. Ethical Considerations of AI and Automation: The growing use of AI and automation raises ethical concerns around bias, openness, and job loss. Addressing these issues through responsible growth, ethical standards, and skills development programs is vital.

3. The Need for Social Protection and Safety Nets: As the nature of work changes, providing social protection and safety nets for people transitioning to new jobs or facing unemployment becomes vital. This might involve measures like national basic income, reskilling programs, and portable benefits.

4. The value of Human Connection and cooperation: While technology gives flexibility and efficiency, the future of work should not ignore the value of human connection and cooperation. Fostering a feeling of

community and connection, even in remote or hybrid work situations, will be crucial for employee well-being and motivation.

5. The Future of Leadership: Leaders in the future of work will need to adapt their approaches to lead successfully in a dynamic and diverse workplace. This includes creating a culture of continuous learning, embracing flexible work models, and valuing employee well-being and mental health.

6. The Role of Policy and Regulation: Governments and lawmakers will need to develop and change policies and laws to handle the challenges and possibilities offered by the future of work. This may involve ensuring fair work practices, supporting digital literacy, and regulating the use of AI and automation in ethical and responsible ways.

By recognizing these nuances and challenges, we can move towards a future of work that is inclusive, sustainable, and helpful for both people and communities.

2. Embracing Flexibility and Adaptability: Thriving in a Dynamic Landscape

The future of work offers a dynamic and ever-evolving world. In this quickly changing environment, the ability to accept flexibility and agility becomes important for people wanting to thrive. Here are some key tactics to cultivate these vital skills:

1. Develop a Growth mentality: Adopt a growth
mentality, thinking that your skills and abilities can be
developed through continuous learning and effort.
This mindset pushes you to accept obstacles as
chances to learn and grow, promoting a more positive
and adaptable approach to change.

2. Cultivate Lifelong Learning: Commit to lifelong
learning, constantly seeking new information and
skills through various paths. This could involve taking
online classes, visiting workshops, engaging in
professional development programs, or simply reading
industry publications. By continuously learning, you
arm yourself with the skills needed to stay relevant in
a changing job market.

3. Embrace New Skills and Technologies: Be open to
learning and acquiring new skills and tools. Don't shy
away from chances to step outside your comfort zone
and discover new areas. This willingness to learn new
things will improve your versatility and keep you
competitive in the changing job market.

4. Develop Transferable Skills: Focus on creating
transferable skills that can be applied across different
jobs and businesses. These skills, such as
communication, critical thinking, problem-solving, and
teamwork, are useful in varied work settings and can
ensure your continuing relevance even in the face of
change.

5. Network and Build Relationships: Build and keep strong business networks. Connect with people from various businesses and subjects, as these links can offer useful insights, new chances, and access to knowledge-sharing platforms.

6. Be Open to New Work Arrangements: Be open to exploring different work arrangements beyond the standard 9-to-5 model. Consider solo or contract work, online work opportunities, or flexible work plans that match with your needs and desires. While not always ideal for everyone, these choices can offer greater flexibility and improve work-life balance.

7. Embrace Continuous growth: View your job as a journey of continuous growth. Regularly assess your skills and explore places for growth. This proactive method allows you to spot possible gaps and actively work towards closing them, ensuring you are constantly evolving and adapting to changing demands

Additional Strategies for Embracing Flexibility and Adaptability:

Sharpen your self-awareness: Regularly think about your skills, weaknesses, hobbies, and beliefs. This self-awareness helps you understand how you fit into the evolving work landscape and find areas for growth that align with your personal job goals.

Develop your critical thought and problem-solving skills: The ability to examine situations, spot problems, and create effective answers will be crucial in navigating the uncertainties of the future of work. Hone these skills by constantly acting in problem-solving activities, participating in critical thought tasks, and challenging your ideas.

Be proactive in getting feedback: Actively seek helpful feedback from peers, teachers, and managers. This feedback can provide useful insights into your strengths and flaws, helping you spot areas for improvement and change your approach accordingly.

Embrace a joint mindset: Collaboration will be key to success in the future of work. Develop strong interpersonal skills, learn to work successfully in teams, and accept different views. This will help you to leverage collective knowledge, solve difficult problems, and add effectively to group tasks.

Learn to handle your time effectively: Time management skills become even more crucial in a dynamic work setting. Develop strategies for prioritizing tasks, handling schedules, and utilizing time efficiently to ensure you meet your goals and stay productive.

Maintain a good work-life balance: Prioritize your physical and mental well-being. Establish healthy limits between job and personal life, participate in stress-relieving activities, and seek help when needed. Maintaining a healthy work-life balance allows you to maintain your energy and focus, promoting endurance and adaptability in the long run.

By adding these additional tactics, people can empower themselves to manage the dynamic future of work with greater confidence and freedom. Remember, the ability to accept change and adapt to new challenges will be an invaluable tool in building a successful and satisfying job in the years to come.

While individual efforts are vital, fostering flexibility and adaptability takes a combined effort:

1. Organizational Support: Organizations can play a vital role by creating a mindset of constant learning and growth. This could involve giving access to training programs, encouraging cross-training opportunities, and supporting skill development through different projects. Additionally, companies can support flexible work arrangements, prioritize employee well-being, and build open communication lines that encourage feedback and adaptation.

2. Government and Policy: Governments can play a vital role by spending in education and training programs that prepare people with the skills needed for the future of work. Additionally, lawmakers can create laws that promote fair labor practices, support ongoing learning programs, and address the possible challenges coming from automation and AI, ensuring a just and inclusive shift into the future of work.

3. Educational Institutions: Educational institutions need to change their curriculums to prepare students for the changing future of work. This may involve incorporating real-world uses into learning, developing critical thinking and problem-solving skills, and promoting adaptability and a growth attitude. Additionally, educational schools can offer lifelong learning chances for people looking to upskill or re-skill throughout their careers.

By accepting flexibility and adaptability, people can not only live but thrive in the dynamic future of work. These skills will allow them to navigate change successfully, seize new chances, and build successful and fulfilling jobs in a constantly evolving world.

3. Opportunities and Challenges of Technological Advancements and Automation: A Double-Edged Sword

Technological developments and robotics are changing nearly every part of our lives, including the world of work. While these advancements present exciting possibilities for improved efficiency, productivity, and innovation, they also raise significant challenges that require careful consideration.

Opportunities:
Increased Efficiency and Productivity:
Reduced Costs: Automation can greatly reduce labor costs, especially in businesses reliant on physical work. This can improve profitability for businesses, possibly leading to lower prices for consumers and greater investment in research and development.

Improved Resource Management: Automation can improve resource usage and scheduling, minimizing waste and increasing productivity. This is important in areas like logistics, manufacturing, and energy generation, leading to better sustainability practices.

24/7 Operations: In specific situations, automation allows for continuous operation without the limits of human weariness or breaks. This can be helpful in areas like healthcare, manufacturing, and customer service, allowing faster response times and uninterrupted service.

Globalized Production and Supply Chains: Automated systems can simplify and align global production and supply chains, allowing faster production cycles, better inventory management, and efficient delivery of goods and services.

Enhanced Innovation and Creativity:
Faster Experimentation and Prototyping: Automation allows for fast prototyping and testing of new ideas and designs, speeding the innovation cycle. This can

lead to quicker product creation, faster market launch, and a competitive edge for companies.

Personalized Products and Services: Automation opens doors to customization and personalization of products and services, responding to individual tastes and needs. This can produce a more customer-centric experience, promoting trust and brand uniqueness.

Enhanced Problem-Solving and Decision-Making: AI and machine learning can examine vast amounts of data to find patterns and trends that humans might miss. This can lead to better insights, informed decision-making, and answers to complicated problems across various areas.

Teamwork between Humans and Machines: Effective human-machine teamwork can maximize the abilities of both groups. Humans can provide creative direction and strategic control, while machines can handle jobs requiring speed, accuracy, and data analysis, leading to a synergistic approach to problem-solving and creativity.

Improved Quality and Accuracy:
Reduced Errors and flaws: Automation reduces human error inherent in repeated tasks, leading to fewer flaws, improved product quality, and enhanced safety in industries like manufacturing and healthcare. This can encourage increased customer trust and confidence in goods and services.

Standardized Work Processes: Automation ensures consistent finishing of tasks according to pre-programmed routines. This standardization reduces variability and ensures uniform quality across production lines and service delivery, leading to reliable outcomes.

Enhanced Quality Control and tracking: Automation allows constant tracking of processes and real-time data collection, allowing for early discovery of errors and possible quality issues. This enables quick remedial action and stops defective goods or services from reaching the end-user.

Improved Data Collection and Analysis: Automated systems can gather and analyze big datasets with greater accuracy and speed compared to human methods. This allows for data-driven decision-making, leading to constant improvement of methods and product quality.

Globalized Workforce and Collaboration:
Access to varied Talent Pool: Technology removes physical obstacles, allowing companies to tap into a bigger pool of talent with varied skills and views. This promotes innovation and creativity by bringing together people with unique backgrounds and knowledge sets.

Improved Communication and Collaboration:
Collaboration tools and platforms enable effective communication and teamwork across physical and

cultural borders. This promotes knowledge sharing, joint problem-solving, and the creation of a truly international and interconnected work environment.

Cultural Exchange and Understanding: Increased global cooperation promotes cultural exchange and understanding, breaking down barriers and promoting tolerance and respect for different viewpoints. This can lead to a more inclusive, collaborative, and interconnected worldwide society.

24/7 Availability and help: With a widely distributed staff, companies can give 24/7 customer help and services. This improves customer happiness and builds brand loyalty by ensuring continuous help and quick settlement of issues.

New Job Creation in the Age of Automation
While the potential for job loss due to technology is a real worry, it is important to recognize the potential for new job creation in different sectors:

1. AI Management and Development: The growing use of AI needs professionals to manage, create, and support these systems. This includes jobs like:
* AI ethicists
* Data security specialists
* AI coders and engineers
* AI trainers and specialists

2. Data Analysis and Interpretation: As data becomes the cornerstone of decision-making across industries, individuals capable of analyzing, understanding, and pulling insights from vast datasets will be in high demand. This includes jobs like:
* Data researchers and scientists
* Business intelligence specialists
* Big data specialists
* Data visualization specialists

3. Human-Machine Cooperation: As technology improves, successful cooperation between people and computers will be crucial. This necessitates people with the ability to:
* Manage and work with AI systems
* Bridge the gap between human and machine skills
* Develop and apply strategies for effective human-machine interaction

4. Automation Specialists: The design, implementation, and care of automated systems will require specialists in different fields, including:
* Robotics engineers and technicians
* Automation process specialists
* Industrial automation engineers

5. Jobs in Emerging Fields: As technology continues to change, entirely new fields and industries may appear, creating unforeseen job possibilities. Staying flexible and open to learning new skills will be crucial to capitalize on these growing possibilities.

It is important to remember that:

The transition to these new possibilities may require upskilling and reskilling programs to equip people with the appropriate skills.

The spread of these new jobs may not be even across all industries and areas, possibly exacerbating existing inequalities.

Focus on education and training is vital to ensure individuals have access to the skills and information needed to thrive in the new job market.

By recognizing both the potential for job loss and the creation of new opportunities, we can aim to create a future of work filled with new possibilities and growth for all.

Challenges:

Challenges of Automation:
1. Job Displacement and Unemployment:
Impact on Specific Sectors: Industries like manufacturing, transportation, and customer service are particularly sensitive to automation, as many jobs can be duplicated by machines with better speed and accuracy. This can lead to major job losses, especially for people with lower levels of education and skills.

Ripple Effect: Job displacement in one sector can have a ripple effect throughout the economy, as it lowers customer spending and demand in other sectors, possibly leading to further job losses.

Income Inequality: Automation can exacerbate income inequality, as the benefits of increased output are often concentrated among a select few, while the negative effects, such as job losses, are felt more widely.

2. Skill Gap and Need for Upskilling:
Rapidly Changing Skills Landscape: As automation takes over regular chores, the demand for new skills, especially those related to technology, critical thought, and problem-solving, will rise. This rapid change can leave people struggling to keep up, possibly leading to unemployment or underemployment.

Cost and Accessibility of Upskilling: Upskilling efforts, such as training programs and educational classes, can be expensive and time-consuming, making them unavailable to certain parts of the population. This can further widen the skills gap and worsen current inequalities.

Psychological Impact: The constant need to learn new skills and adapt to change can lead to worry, stress, and feelings of inadequacy among workers, possibly impacting their well-being and productivity.

Addressing these issues is crucial to ensure that the benefits of automation are generally shared and that everyone can thrive in the changing world of work.

3. Ethical Concerns of Automation:
Bias, Transparency, and Accountability:
Bias in Algorithmic Design: AI algorithms are taught on data sets that may reflect social biases, leading them to spread discrimination against certain groups in areas like jobs, loan approvals, and criminal justice. This can have major negative effects for people and communities.

Lack of Transparency: The inner workings of complex AI systems are often shrouded in secret, making it difficult to understand how decisions are made and hold creators or users responsible for biased or unfair results.

Unintentional Harm: Unforeseen flaws in algorithms can lead to unintentional harm, such as continuing racial profiling or increasing misinformation.

4. Inequality and Social Disruption:
Unequal Distribution of Benefits: The benefits of technology and AI may not be shared fairly. Wealthy people and developed countries may have better access to the resources and skills needed to adjust to new technologies, while others may be left behind, further widening the gap between the "haves" and "have-nots."

Social Disruption: Rapid technological change can lead to social disruption, as people and groups fight to adapt to new realities. This can have effects for social cohesion, trust in organizations, and general community well-being.

Need for Policy Interventions: Addressing these concerns requires proactive policy interventions, such as regulations to mitigate bias in algorithms, promote transparency and accountability, and ensure inclusive access to education and skills training to help everyone benefit from technological progress.

5. The Future of Work: Challenges and Opportunities
The transformation driven by automation and changing technologies offers both obstacles and possibilities for the future of work. While concerns about job stability, work-life balance, and human connection are real, we can navigate these changes by prioritizing human well-being and creating a sense of meaning and satisfaction.

Challenges and Concerns:
Job Security: As technology changes current jobs, individuals may face worries about job security and the ability to find new opportunities, especially those with old skills.

Work-Life Balance: Technological developments can blur the lines between work and personal life, possibly leading to longer work hours, burnout, and decreased well-being.
Human Connection and Social Interaction: Increased dependence on technology and automation could lead to social isolation and a decrease in face-to-face

exchanges, affecting personal satisfaction and social unity.

Opportunities and Strategies:
Investing in Upskilling and Education: By offering open and cheap chances for constant learning and skills development, people can adapt to the changing job market and secure satisfying careers.

Pushing Work-Life Balance: Encouraging flexible work plans, pushing digital wellness practices, and setting clear limits between work and personal life can help keep a healthy balance.

Human-Centered Design: Technology should be built with human needs and well-being in mind, supporting teamwork, innovation, and important social relationships in the workplace.

Universal Basic Income (UBI): This idea suggests a guaranteed income for all people, regardless of work status, and could provide a safety net for individuals managing job loss or finding new opportunities.

Focus on Human-Machine Collaboration: Instead of viewing automation as a replacement, it should be seen as a tool to enhance human skills, allowing people to focus on tasks that require imagination, critical thought, and social intelligence.
Creating a Future of Work that Prioritizes Human Well-being:

Building a future of work that values human well-being takes a collaborative effort from people, groups, and policymakers. By investing in education and skills training, supporting healthy work practices, fostering human-centered technology, and exploring new solutions like UBI, we can build a future where everyone can thrive in a fast changing world.

Ultimately, the future of work is not predetermined. Through proactive planning, ethical considerations, and continuous adaptation, we can shape a future where technology empowers people, supports useful work, and adds to a society focused on well-being and human potential.

By recognizing both the possibilities and challenges provided by technological advancements and automation, we can develop strategies to harness the positive potential of these advancements while mitigating their negative effects. This will take a joint effort from people, groups, lawmakers, and educational institutions to build a future of work that is inclusive, sustainable, and useful for all.

Conclusion:

In the pages of "Escape the 9-5: Embrace the Part-Time Revolution," we've started on a journey of discovery, freedom, and change. We've studied the limitations of the standard 9-5 work model and revealed the boundless potential of accepting part-time employment.

Throughout this book, we've looked into the evolution of work culture, the reasons behind the rise of part-time employment, and the various benefits and challenges associated with flexible work arrangements. We've celebrated the freedom, flexibility, and satisfaction that part-time work offers, and we've equipped ourselves with the tools and insights needed to manage this brave new world of work.

But beyond the insights and knowledge learned, this book is a rousing cry. It's a call to action for each and every one of us to break free from the limits of conventional advice and forge our own paths to success. It's a reminder that we have the power to create our jobs, our lives, and our futures on our own terms.

As we end the chapter on "Escape the 9-5: Embrace the Part-Time Revolution," let us bring forth the spirit of creativity, adaptability, and resiliency that defines this movement. Let us dare to dream of a world where work is not a burden but a source of joy, where every person has the freedom to follow their interests and live life to the best.

So, as you start on your own journey towards part-time empowerment, remember this: the Part-Time Revolution is not just a trend – it's a paradigm change. It's a declaration of freedom, a celebration of autonomy, and a testament to the endless possibilities that await when we dare to challenge tradition.

Embrace the Part-Time Revolution. Embrace flexibility. Embrace freedom. Your road to a more fulfilling job starts now.

Here's a review of the key lessons from the book

1. Rethink Traditional Work Models: The book questions the traditional 9-5 work model and encourages readers to explore alternative options, such as part-time jobs, that offer greater freedom and work-life balance.

2. Evolution of Work Culture: It discusses the evolution of work culture over time, highlighting the change towards flexible work arrangements and the reasons behind the rise of part-time jobs.

3. Benefits of Part-Time Work: Part-time employment offers numerous benefits, including freedom, work-life

blending, various possibilities, decreased stress, and personal growth.

4. Challenges of Part-Time Work: Despite its benefits, part-time work also presents challenges such as limited benefits, pay uncertainty, job growth obstacles, and social isolation.

5. Welcome the Part-Time Revolution: The book urges readers to welcome the Part-Time Revolution and achieve a satisfying job on their own terms. It stresses the importance of pushing for flexible work arrangements and sharing success stories to inspire others.

Embracing the Part-Time Revolution is not just about getting a job – it's about finding satisfaction, balance, and joy in your work and your life. It's about reclaiming power over your time, your goals, and your fate.

So, I urge you to step bravely into this new frontier of flexible work arrangements. Embrace the freedom to create a job that aligns with your interests, values, and goals. Whether you're seeking more time for family, following a creative project, or simply craving a better work-life balance, part-time employment offers endless possibilities for personal and professional satisfaction.

Don't settle for the status quo. Don't resign yourself to a life of burnout, stress, and unhappiness. You deserve more – more freedom, more control, more happiness. And the Part-Time Revolution is your ticket to getting it.

So, take the leap. Explore new chances, try with different plans, and dare to dream of a job that improves your life rather than depletes it. Your journey to a more fulfilling job starts now – are you ready to accept it?

Join the drive towards flexible work arrangements and be a part of changing the future of work! Your experiences, ideas, and success stories have the power to inspire and empower others to join the Part-Time Revolution.

Share your journey with us. Whether you've found fulfillment in a part-time job, overcome obstacles, or discovered new chances for growth, your story counts. By sharing your stories, you can help break down obstacles, question stereotypes, and show the value of flexible work arrangements.

Together, let's build a community of support, encouragement, and lobbying for part-time work. Let's amplify our voices, share our knowledge, and support the benefits of flexibility in the workplace.

So, I ask you to share your part-time success stories, tips, and thoughts with others. Whether through social media, online groups, or in-person talks, let's start conversations, inspire change, and create a future where everyone has the chance to pursue a satisfying job on their own terms.

Join us in the Part-Time Revolution – together, we can make flexible work plans the standard, not the exception.